WOKINGHAM
the town of my life

By Ken Goatley

I dedicate this book to my dear wife Edna who has supported and assisted me in all that I have been involved with in Wokingham. This story will show how our lives have been entwined for many years. Any small thing that I have achieved has been with her full support.

Printed and bound in Great Britain
by Conservatree Print and Design, Reading.

ISBN No. 0 9534735 9 7

Acknowledgements.

I must express my sincere thanks and gratitude to my good friend Jim Bell who has been a stalwart ally in editing this book and has dealt with the illustrations with seemingly great ease. He has also devoted many hours on this project. Without Jim this book would never have been completed.

oOo

A thank you to friends at the Wokingham Society who have commented on the initial text and made excellent suggestions—a dedicated effort.

oOo

I am indebted also to Peter Dawkes, "Studio Carr", for the cover illustration. Peter and I met quite by chance one Sunday morning and he took this photograph which seems to me to be absolutely ideal for the purpose.

oOo

Finally my grateful thanks to the Wokingham Society which has looked favourably upon this publication by providing a grant from the J. H. Elliston Clifton Fund for the printing of the book. All proceeds from the sales of this work will go to the current Mayor's Charity. It is hoped that many will benefit.

oOo

Grateful thanks to all authors and owners of photographs known and unknown.
K. G.

Contents

Illustrations

Foreword

The history that we were taught in school or have read since was usually about kings and queens, politicians and laws, battles and wars. Some of it was probably true. Other parts were certainly not the whole truth - being written by the victors.

Social history has come into its own in the last seventy years. Those who have lived through this period in the UK are conscious of the many changes that have occurred in the way we work, live and play. Transport, retail trade, health care, provision for the elderly, education, the development of television and mobile phones - what has stayed the same since the thirties? Books like this which paint a picture of life as it was bring home to us all that has changed. In another hundred years this book will be a sourcebook for students painting a picture of a town which will seem so remote.

One of the most significant features of life in the thirties is not spelt out but shines through the text. Wokingham was a community, small and isolated enough for the townsfolk to be conscious of each other. There were social divisions but everyone knew and was known by almost everyone else. Now we have a vastly expanded population of which few were born here and many of whom are merely transient residents. The town is poorer in that way but for ex-city dwellers it still has some of the air of a centre of community. Is it a happier place than it was? Reading the book gives the impression that we have lost out. Perhaps that is because its author has a sunny disposition and remembers the happy times more than the sad ones.

Ken Goatley has known Wokingham for longer than most of us. He was born here and is the authority for all that has happened since. Together with his wife Edna he has regaled countless audiences with his memories and pictures of Wokingham. Those who have heard him talk will remember not only the details of life in the thirties and the relics of earlier times which were still about then, but the enthusiasm with which he talked - he enjoyed the telling as much as the audience delighted in the hearing. Now we can enjoy his gathered memories expressed in print with the same fascinating detail and boundless enthusiasm.
Thanks Ken!

Donald Macdonald, for The Wokingham Society.

Wokingham—A Market Town.

A very long history is attributed to Wokingham, although not named as such at the time. It is well documented that a settlement was established here by members of the Saxon tribe of the Uuoccinghas (Wocckingas). It is not my intention to dwell upon this period of the town's history as it would probably result with the reader putting this booklet down immediately. However, I do believe that it is worth mentioning how Wokingham became a market town and why.

In the 13th century the bishopric of Sonning, which included Wokingham, was in the control of the Bishop of Salisbury, and history tells us that there was a need to move the location of Salisbury Cathedral, so funds were needed to build the new edifice.

A decision was made to purchase three market charters from King Henry III, because market towns would raise a great deal of money for the cause. The chosen locations were Salisbury, Ramsbury and Wokingham. So the Bishop went ahead with this plan and a charter for Wokingham was purchased with a palfrey. ("A what?", I hear you ask. It's a lady's riding horse). At this time in 1219 the King was only a boy of 13 years and the charter was formally ratified in 1227 upon the King coming of age. The charter actually stated that a market could be held peaceably every Tuesday. Other Charters have been presented over the years. Details of these are available in various documents.

One assumes that a similar situation applied to the other two locations. Salisbury of course was very successful and has become an historic city. Ramsbury was not a great success and now has become little more than a village. I think it is fair to say that Wokingham has been quite successful and is still thriving despite all the gloom and doom by some factions of the community. It has gone through many dark periods and has also been deemed in the past to have been a major centre for the sports of bull-baiting in the Market Place and cock-fighting (Cockpit Path!).

However, the original plan must have been thought to be a success because work began on the new cathedral in 1220.

There were parts of Wokingham still in the control of a Wiltshire estate, the hundred of Amesbury, until 1845. This included the church of All Saints which had been dedicated in 1193 by Hubert, Bishop of Salisbury when he became Archbishop of Canterbury. In 1845 all the areas of land in and around Wokingham that had been in the control of Wiltshire finally became Berkshire land.

The town has had various bodies controlling its business over the centuries. For a period up until 1885 it was in the control of an Alderman—an all powerful man with his burgesses sitting in council. Then in that year the Victorian Charter changed the constitution and Wokingham's first Mayor, Thomas Manley Wescott, resigned his position as Alderman to take up the new office. This form of local government continued until 1974 when many Borough Councils were abolished and, as in the case of Wokingham, became town councils. At a special court held at Windsor Castle in 1975, Queen Elizabeth II authorised, by Order of Council, that the Armorial Bearings (Coat of Arms) granted to Wokingham in 1953 to be *"lawfully borne and used"*. Wokingham has been able to continue with a Mayor and also use all its insignia, whereas many former boroughs now display the mace etc. in a showcase at a local museum.

I hope that has given some idea of what the town is about. I know that there is a great deal of information available on this subject, so I feel there is little point in too much repetition.

oOo

The Early Years.

Life in Wokingham began for me in February, 1927 at No.86 Wescott Road. My parents must have had a room or rooms for a time early in their married life. A modest start, which in all honesty, has been a fairly modest life.

Mother and me at 86 Westcott Road.

Thinking back to Wescott Road and my first home, the area that includes No.86 is the narrow part leading down to London Road. This has always been known as the 'Cinder Track'. Many of the houses here have been modernised externally and internally but in general the scene has changed very little and there is no doubt that the people who live there today are still the friendly people of Wokingham that they always were.

As was usually the case at that time, I was taken to church for baptism at a very early age. This was performed by Canon Bertram Long, Rector at All Saints Church, who went through all the usual procedures before dubbing me Kenneth William John. It could have been much worse.

An early incident in my life concerned a dog. This rather large and fearsome animal was owned by Mrs. Sleet who lived at No.90. The dog was housed in a large kennel in the yard at the rear and by all accounts I would crawl into this kennel and gnaw on the hoard of bones that the dog had there. He would not let anyone near the kennel to get me out so it was a case of waiting patiently, and no doubt worryingly, for me to make my exit, none the worse for the experience.

Whilst living in Wescott Road, my parents made some very good friends, in particular Mr. and Mrs. Chapman, living at No.92 who I always knew as Auntie and Uncle Chapman. I never used their Christian names of Charlie and Emily. As a small boy I was dressed as a page-boy for the wedding of their daughter Florrie to George Lovejoy. What an embarrassment!!

I remember the Englefield family living at No.94 with much affection. Somehow we lost touch and drifted apart. I suppose that's the way life is.

Wescott Road and the immediate locality has changed very little, unlike many parts of the town. But it is sad to think back on the lost small shops—Mr. Hall and his family in the little corner sweet shop across the road from the school. Almost opposite was the small grocery shop of Annie and Emily Beale, the coal business of Mr. Street and the business of Mr. Nicholls who sold household goods and, of course, paraffin oil. At that time this was quite a much used product both for heating and, in some cases, lighting.

The Council School in Wescott Road was opened in 1906 and, like the road, was named after Thomas Manley Wescott, the first Borough Mayor. It has always seemed rather odd that some children in that area went to either Palmer School, that is the original Palmer where now stands Meachen Court, or even St. Paul's school, whilst children from Rose Street, Denmark Street and other areas attended Wescott. It has been said that they were probably sent where one or other of their parents attended school. That may be the solution, but it still seems rather odd. It is quite likely that children went where there was a vacancy.

It is certain that children from all the schools in the area attended woodwork lessons and cookery lessons in the separate building in the Wescott Road school playground. The carpentry instructor was Mr. Heath and the cookery teacher was Miss Jones. Certainly these periods were a welcome change to the normal classroom lessons.

Dad on Painter's motorised tri-bike.

At the time we were living in Wescott Road, my father would have been employed by Painter the butcher/fishmonger in Denmark Street. Later it became the business of Gosling. He had a rather large three wheeled vehicle fitted with a small engine and a box arrangement on the front. It must have been difficult to ride. After that he then became a milkman for The Creamery in Peach Street.

I am not certain when we moved from Wescott Road into Langborough Road, but we then lived in the first floor flat of No. 32—a building in the ownership of the Salvation Army. How this letting was acquired I have no idea, but I vividly recall that at the time my father was still working for The Creamery. He delivered milk around the town in a covered trap pulled by a pony.

5

Dad always dressed very smartly in a slate grey uniform wearing a peaked cap and polished leather gaiters. I can remember very clearly that he would call home for a cup of tea when in Langborough Road. Then he would take me out, stand me in front of him, give me the reins and I would drive the trap up to the end of Howard Road. How important I must have felt. Then I was put off the trap to return home—a short distance along the road.

Dad with Creamery pony and trap.

In later years he returned to the butchery trade where he spent his working life. After The Creamery, he worked for Sidney Pither in Broad Street. He spent many years in this employment and I well remember the many late nights and early mornings as Christmas approached. There were no frozen turkeys etc. at that time and all the staff at the butcher shops around the town spent many hours killing and plucking turkeys. They were then trussed before delivery to all the customers over a very wide area.

The slaughter house at the rear of what is now the Newbury Building Society premises has been replaced by a new development. It is proposed to turn this into a retail unit. It was here that all the poultry preparation took place. My father told me on many occasions that one of his colleagues at that time was so swift that he could kill a bird and have it plucked before the nerves had ceased twitching. Some feat!

No.9 Rose Street, The Eagle Public House.
Queen's Terrace on left.

In 1931 we moved from Langborough Road into Rose Street. The Eagle public house had closed, apparently to take up a full licence on The Plough in London Road. The Wesleyan Chapel, as it was at that time, had the opportunity to purchase the property which was their next door neighbour. They made the most of the chance to eliminate the noise of the lads and lasses in the yard beside the church joining in with the hymn singing,

Although I was only four years old at that time I have vivid memories of the event. I recall the large pile of empty bottles outside the window in the yard. There must have been hundreds.

What did they do with them? Also, there was an entrance porch just inside the front door to separate the bars. I remember my uncle, Cecil Case, taking a sledgehammer to that and quickly demolishing it. He also pulled up large square cut wall nails that had been used to fix the linoleum. His comments about the perpetrator of that deed cannot be repeated here.

There must have been a mountain of work to transform the pub into a family home. However, it happened and we settled down to a pleasant way of life. Mr. John Hopkins, was the owner of the wheelwright's yard, at that time located in Cross Street—not the street we know today, but the road that ran in a straight line from Rose Street to Peach Street.

Anyway back to John Hopkins. He was a very small gentleman who drove quite a large car about the town and viewed the road ahead through the spars of his steering wheel. He also smoked a pipe, the aroma of which lasted for hours after a visit, and visit he did regularly every Monday morning to collect the rent for this eight roomed house.

The house also had a scullery, two toilets outside, a brick building which had formerly been stables, a coal cellar and an enclosed area for the dustbins in the dry, very large cellar under the house. Remember it had been a pub and there was a large backyard. All this was rented at the princely sum of five shillings (25p) per week.

Dad, Mum, me and sister Joyce.

8

In the latter part of the year of the move we had an addition to the family. My sister Joyce was born. So Mum and Dad were now blessed with a 'pigeon pair'. I'm not at all sure that they felt blessed at times.

As a family we were always very happy at No.9 but of course as was the norm at that time there were a number of things that would not be acceptable to people today.

Toilet facilities, as mentioned, were outside. Having been a public house there was the advantage of two WCs—formerly the ladies and gents. The additional thing that would not be acceptable to people today was the toilet paper. Almost without exception in working class households this would have been yesterday's newspaper cut into squares, a hole bored in one corner, threaded on a piece of string and hung on a nail in the wall. At night-time the illumination would be provided by a candle or perhaps the luxury of a torch. The real luxury came with the winter months when there was a danger of freezing pipes. An oil stove would then be put in the toilet—'snug as a bug in a rug'.

The house had gas for cooking and lighting in the downstairs rooms, but not upstairs, which either had to be illuminated by oil lamps or candles. The gas lights on the lower floor were fitted with mantles. These were small hanging cases of a fine net material which, after fitting and lit for use, became very flimsy indeed. The slightest touch and they fell to pieces. For instance if a moth flew into the glass cover and touched the mantle, that was the end of it.

Electricity was installed some years later—what a boon!! Heating was by coal fires. Six of the eight rooms had fireplaces, two of the bedrooms did not and, if the need arose, an oil stove would be used. The room where we spent most of the time had a kitchen range. That comprised an open fire plus an oven. This was quite common in homes at that time and the housewives could judge the heat of the oven when cooking and baking by putting their hand in to test the temperature. It was a practised art.

The 'front room', as it was always referred to, was set aside for special days, Sundays and days when guests were entertained. This contained a three-piece suite and was carpeted. A glass cabinet

9

with china pieces graced one wall, the piano another. It was always an event when we had a fire in the front room.

A good stock of coal was, of course, a necessity, and deliveries were made on a regular basis. Most of the coalmen were honest chaps, but there were occasions when the odd rogue would try to make himself a little extra by cheating on the delivery thus gaining a sack of coal to sell elsewhere. This was achieved by piling the empty sacks on the ground by the cart as each was emptied and it was a simple matter to take an empty sack off the cart and add to the pile. If queried, he would count the sacks to prove how many had been delivered. Most housewives—and mother was one of them—would watch the delivery making sure the coalman knew he was being surveyed. The budget was too tight to lose cash in that way.

These coal fires created a good deal of soot in the chimneys and it was necessary to have the chimney sweep in every few months to deal with this. At that time there were no vacuums used by the sweeps and indeed, had there been, there was often no electricity in the home. It was a day's work to prepare the room with covers etc., have the chimney swept and then clean up the inevitable coating of soot afterwards. Life was hard for the housewives in many ways. We children were always told by the sweep to go outside and let him know when the brush came out of the chimney. This made us feel very important. Of course he knew when this had been achieved without our help, but it did get us out of the way!

As in many working class homes having a bath was quite a performance. We had a long zinc bath which would be filled with kettles of hot water and cold added to achieve the right temperature, then we children would take it in turns to bathe, put on night clothes and off to bed, having been given the usual potion of senna-pods which had been brewing on the kitchen range, absolutely vile! Presumably our parents followed this routine (without the brew) but of course we never witnessed it. Some years later the former larder, which was quite large and able to take a full sized bath, was installed with a gas geyser for hot water, not only much more convenient but provided privacy too.

Opposite our home in Rose Street stood the three houses erected by Isaiah Gadd at the beginning of the 1900s, named '*Wesley House*', '*to St.John*' and '*of Epworth*'. I have a vivid memory of standing at the attic window (arrowed) of 'Epworth', the home of Mr. and Mrs. Lawrence, watching over the rooftops the tremendous fire at Mr. Bill Denton's chair factory which was completely destroyed. Many years later in April 1960, the Wokingham Plastics factory was destroyed by fire on the same site. Today the fire station is located there so there should not be a recurrence.

Isaiah Gadd's houses in Rose Street.

The Bush Tuesday Market.

As I mentioned in the introduction, the market was to be held on a Tuesday. What is not stated is the location. For many years the Market Place was a car park for much of the week, but on Tuesday

Mr. Butler, an auctioneer from Reading, held a regular market at the rear of the Bush Hotel. His voice could be clearly heard in Rose Street as he dealt with the various items for sale. Much of this was livestock, chickens, other poultry, rabbits and a wide variety of implements. So in that respect the conditions of the Market Charter were upheld.

It was from 9 Rose Street that I started school. Palmer School at that time was a very short distance from home, just through Rose Court. On my very first day we were sent out from class and I headed straight home and dashed through the back gate to be met by mother hanging washing on the clothes line. "Why have you come home?", she said. I must have said something like, "I have come home for dinner". She told me that it was play-time not dinner time and by the time she reached the gate I had disappeared into Rose Court and back to school.

Like many other pupils at Palmer I remember with much affection, Miss Goodship, the teacher. In the very early class she placed the letters of the alphabet around the room and had us recite after her what now seem to be very strange pronunciations. It must have worked because we learned. I wonder how many times in her life that dear lady had gone through that routine. Miss Jones was the other teacher in the infant school and although kindly enough, a little firmer with the children than Miss Goodship.

Palmer School 1875-1972

Having been initiated into the school by these two kindly ladies, many of the former pupils will remember the next teacher we encountered. Moving out of the infants we came face to face with Miss Bromley—to say the least, a formidable lady..

The senior school with classes ranged from Standard 1 to Standard 7. Each class had a different teacher, some of them seeming to have been there forever. In my early years the Headmaster was Mr. Maidment and, when he retired, Mr. Eagles came to the school as Headmaster. Both of these gentlemen were kindly, but firm, schoolmasters.

One of the wonderful occasions at school was the day of the Christmas Tree. The Main Room, as it was known, was in fact two classrooms separated by a heavy curtain on a rail. This could be pushed back to make a reasonably sized hall and at Christmas time a very large tree was erected, beautifully decorated with many presents around the base. I expect, in fact, that they only included the infant classes, but in honesty I cannot be sure.

However, we all sat with bated breath being kept very quiet until we heard the sleigh bells ringing on the roof. Santa would appear at one of the high windows, climb through and descend a ladder very conveniently placed. He would then read out the names on the parcels and we would eagerly collect our present from him—magic!!

It was quite some while before I learned that Santa was in fact one of the school governors, Mr. David Goddard. He was a gentleman who many of us boys received much benefit from when he formed a youth club. Comments on that later.

There is another little story in relation to the Christmas Tree. My sister Joyce, in her very early infant school days, was sick and away from school at the time the children wrote their letters for presents. The consequence was that although she was at the party for the tree presents, unfortunately she had been overlooked. To compensate, she was then presented with the fairy doll off the top of the tree. To this day some 66 years later that same doll sits on top of their family Christmas Tree, having been re-dressed once or twice.

I recall with some pride that, at Palmer, and also at the other schools in the town, we celebrated Empire Day, May 24th. We all gathered in the playground with many parents present. We would sing patriotic songs such as, "I vow to thee my country" and "Land of hope and glory", and march around the playground passing the flagstaff bearing the Union Flag, or as most people refer to it— the Union Jack. A lovely memory. Today we have no Empire.

That same playground saw children having hours of happy playtimes. The girls were in a separate area to the boys and consequently football dominated the boys' playground. There was always a tennis ball that someone had brought to school and sides just seemed to form and some very hectic and sometimes quite rough play took place. But all very enjoyable.

It is rather odd that in the dinner hour the football would take place in the road outside. Well, I say road, but really what was there at that time was just a sandy gravel strip—but it provided ample space for a goal at each end and a good sized playing area.

Although I went home for dinner, being only a few minutes from the school, I was always keen to get back as soon as I possibly could to join in the football. We were certainly a keen bunch. This road today is a well surfaced tarmac road in front of Meachen Court (Mr. Sid Meachen was the last Headmaster at the school). It is also the service road to the Waitrose store.

The days that most of the children did not like was when we had a surprise visit from Nurse Hessay. Probably the staff knew of her coming, but certainly the pupils had no idea. The nurse would call each one into the Headmaster's study and examine nails, hair and teeth—especially teeth. If anyone had a loose tooth, they would stand in the queue waggling it about hoping to dislodge it before Nurse Hessay could pull it for them—which she did without hesitation. If it became necessary, the pupil would be referred to the school dentist. What an experience.

The dentist operated in the old clinic which was on the site of the present Red Cross Centre in Denmark Street and his dentistry tools had to be seen to be believed. If a filling was needed he had this machine which he treadled with one foot while at the same time drilling the tooth. It had to be experienced—horrific!!

We all progressed steadily through the various stages of our education. In truth, we were a rather mixed bunch, some of which must have caused the teaching staff many heartaches and headaches. During the war years many of the local male teachers were called into the armed forces and, to fill the gaps, some retired teachers were recalled into the profession.

One of these was a lady named Mrs. Peters. She appeared to us to be a rather formidable lady, dressed in a tweed suit and with a very stern appearance. In fact she was a kindly person and her one great passion was gardening.

As the nation was being extolled to 'Dig for Victory!', it was arranged for the school to cultivate the garden of the Rectory (now the site of Suffolk Lodge) in Rectory Road, the home of Reverend Gordon Kenworthy. By this time I and my classmates had become senior members of the school so we were the allotted gardeners—much against the grain in my case. Mrs. Peters would take us along and guide us in our duties. Her one great slogan was 'Never dig for brassica'. In other words the ground needed to be kept firm for the cabbages etc., to root. Having been quite successful in our efforts we had quite a crop of vegetables.

Then came the part that I was quite happy with. Gordon, a classmate, and myself were delegated as 'gardening boys' and it was our duty to go round all the classes prior to the weekend to tell the pupils and staff what was available. Some teachers frowned upon these interruptions. We then had to follow this up the next day to collect orders from the pupils—more frowns, follow this up by cropping, weighing and bagging, then deliver to the classrooms. Yet more frowns, but the two of us enjoyed this out of class activity.

During my years at school we did not have school dinners. Children that came some distance brought sandwiches and those living nearby went home for their mid-day meal. What we did have was school milk. This came in small third of a pint bottles and cost twopence-halfpenny a week—roughly equivalent to 1p today. If desired in the cold weather, the milk monitor would place the bottles on the classroom's Victorian style radiators to warm—a small treat.

In some respects I may have been a little unfortunate with my education. When I was at the age to take the examinations for attendance at Ranelagh School, our home was stricken with measles. The consequence of this was that I was unable to attend school at the time of the exams. In those days there was only the one period in one's schooling to take the exams. I am not sure that it worried me unduly but certainly the Headmaster at that time expressed his disappointment to me and stated that he felt sure I could have passed with flying colours. Who knows? I have certainly enjoyed my life with just the backing of an elementary education.

Whilst I was still at school mother decided that I should have pianoforte lessons and, every week, I went dutifully along to Miss Adey—a sweet little elderly lady who lived in a flat above No.8, Denmark Street. She was very patient but she was also very astute. She knew very well that for me to go home and practice what she had taught me was out of the question. Putting the music case down and out with the boys to play football was more my way of life. Edna was taking lessons at the same time and, as she came up the stairs, I was going down. It must be said that her progress was very much better than mine. In my case it really was a sinful waste of hard earned cash.

There were two occasions which former Palmer School pupils found richly rewarding. During the 1990s two people, Joyce (Smith) Lee and Ray Reed, with a small committee, set to work to arrange a school reunion. It was a great success. Other people pitched in to supply refreshments and the hall at the Palmer School in Norreys Avenue was packed to capacity. Amazingly one of our former masters put in an appearance. Mr. Pitt, very aged, but delighted to be present, as we all were, to see him again. All the school record books were on display and many pictures of football teams and other events.

Music was supplied, and dancing and socialising were the order of the day. It was such a great evening that another reunion was arranged and that also went very well. Sadly, nobody was prepared to take on the job of further events so those two evenings were all that were held, but still a very happy memory.

An incident that I clearly recall from my very early years was a cricket match at the London Road cricket ground, which was located on land belonging to the Norreys farm. Going into Barrett Crescent, as it is today, from the London Road, the ground would have been off to the left. Anyway, as a very young boy I sat on the boundary—the lone spectator. At the tea interval the local skipper came over to me and said, "Come on son, have some tea". He escorted me into the pavilion and I was fed quite royally on sandwiches, cakes etc.—then back to the field to watch the remainder of the match.

Many years later when I was treasurer of St. Sebastian's Football Club, I was informed by Bert Forester, a local man, that the Council wished to clear the site of the dressing room/pavilion at Barrett Crescent and advised me to make a bid for the building. I sent a letter offering £25 which was accepted.

The players at the club banded together and dismantled the wooden building. With the assistance of Bob Palterman with his farming families flat bed trailer and tractor, the whole lot was transported to the playing field at St. Sebastian's. A hard working gang of enthusiasts, ably led by Dave Simonds, re-erected the pavilion adding toilets, showers and a kitchen. It was luxury indeed! Some years later the whole was demolished and redeveloped by the council with a brick building which is used by various clubs etc.

It was on that same ground in London Road that a circus big-top was erected. My long suffering wife Edna and I, as young children, were given sixpence each to visit the circus. I, as the dominant male, was given the money to carry. Unfortunately I lost one of the sixpences, so I promptly sent Edna home and went to the circus alone. Yet she married me many years later. Women never learn.

A short distance from this field, on the Binfield Road, and almost directly opposite the end of Barrett Crescent, was Equals Pond—real adventure playground for kids. About two thirds distance across the pond was a fence which we never ventured beyond, but many happy hours were spent there seeking sticklebacks, minnows and newts of all varieties. Now of course it is a pathway and somebody's frontage.

Living next door to the Wesleyan Chapel it was inevitable that events occurred that tied in with that. At eight years of age I joined the 5th Wokingham Cub Pack under the leadership of Miss Locke and Molly Douglas. Many boys of my age joined at the same time. On the very first evening we were taken down to All Saints Church to climb the tower to view the bells being rung, and also take in the view from the top—quite an adventure. That is the one and only time that I have been up the church tower in my life. However I did rise to the giddy heights of being a 'sixer' in the Pack.

In the schoolroom, still used, but soon to be demolished to make way for the new development, at the Wesleyan it was possible, on the payment of one or two pennies, to have an evening of entertainment watching lantern slides. I believe it was Miss West and Miss Walker, both from Murdoch Road, that showed slides of wild birds. There was also an elderly gentleman that gave a similar show. It all seemed quite magical at the time. Edna and I sometimes reflect on this and wonder if the children we have visited at schools, to show the slides of Wokingham, will in future years say, "Do you remember that old man and woman that used to show pictures of Wokingham?"

At the rear of the chapel was a green corrugated tin building furnished with long wooden forms for seating. It was here that I attended Sunday School. Alternatively, Sunday School lessons were also held at the Palmer Schools.

When I was a lad in Rose Street, the church organ at the Wesleyan was hand pumped and the organist for some years was Miss Coombs, from Billingbear. She would cycle in to practice on a Saturday morning and would pay Jack Rance, living on the other side of the chapel, and myself threepence each to pump the organ for her.

We would pump away until the weight was at its highest point then, being the rascals we were, we would place a hymn book at each end of the aisle and with a tennis ball, use it as a bowling alley. It was, of course, inevitable that the organ would run out of 'puff' whilst we were so engaged and would almost groan to a stop. Miss Coombs would look down from her high perch whilst we pumped furiously to put matters to rights. I don't know why she tolerated us.

Nos. 5 and 7 Rose Street. Jack Rance lived at No. 7 next door to the church.

Having mentioned Jack Rance, he was errand boy for Mr. Rawlings a grocer in the Market Place two doors along from the Red Lion. Jack was going away for a few days and he suggested to Mr. Rawlings that I should do his round on the Saturday. Now I have never been in any way a big strong boy and, here I was confronted by a large trades-bike, and on the front a very large basket loaded with groceries. Ride it? I had a difficult task pushing it. Somewhere in the Cockpit Path/Howard Road area the load overpowered me and the whole lot tumbled out across the road. Somebody must have picked it up and sorted it. Certainly it was the end of my errand boy days.

Throughout my life I have read, or had related to me, what a terrible place Rose Street was. It would seem that it was almost life threatening to even walk down there. I am not talking about the dark ages. These tales come from people living in the town today. In fact, very recently in 2003, I was told that this was the case as the teller recalled it. How does one respond to this? It is very simple—"utter rubbish", "balderdash", and any other such term that comes to mind. Having lived in the street, from a young age until my middle twenties, I can say with every confidence that it was a very happy place to be.

It was almost a self-contained village. In the thirties there were a number of business premises. Going from the top of the street was Wimbledon's Garage; then Nos. 16/18 Frank Knight, plumber and selling all sanitary ware; at No. 32a was the shop of Philip Stratton selling cigarettes, groceries and confectionery. Next to Rose Court was the shoe repair shop of Fred Lee. He rarely labelled the repairs and the customers would have to identify their own shoes. Still on that side The Metropolitan public house—still very much in business today. This is quite amazing considering the huge losses they must have suffered at this time by the youngsters taking bottles from the yard at the rear and collecting pennies on 'returns' at the off-licence.

At No. 70, the small general stores of Alfred Swain; at No. 72, the business of Robert Yalden, undertaker; at No. 80, Harold Smith, greengrocer; finally on that side of the road at No. 82/84, the premises of William Hallworth baker, plus oats, bran, corn etc. In the building, at the rear, the cows from Elms Field would be milked. One of the great delights at this bakery, small brown loaves at a penny each taken home hot, spread with butter—delicious.

Crossing the road, and moving back up to just below Queens Terrace at No.11, was the coalyard of Talbot's; at No. 23, The Queen's Arms public house; at No.27, the shop of Miss Prust—a lady who always wore a beret, and without fail had a cigarette in her mouth. She was partnered by Miss Caiger in running this shop which was directly opposite Rose Court and many children would buy their sweets here on their way to school.

Next door was the fish and chip shop of Mrs. Johnson, a 'pennorth' of chips and a farthingsworth of crackling (small pieces of batter that had broken off—delicious!).

There were two professional chimney sweeps living in Rose Street, Tom Green living at No.31 (formerly the home of James "Sooty" Seaward) and Manny Rose who lived at No. 65.

Fred Lee's repair shop. (Rose Court on right).

Left to right Tom Green's cottage; fish and chip shop and Miss Prust's sweet shop.

Families at that time were almost all working-class living in rented accommodation, but they were hard working, happy people. The children played in the street often until it was too dark to see properly by the light rendered from the gas lights. These would be lit by the two lamp-lighters, Mr. Brooks and George Kingston.

It was in the dusk of evening that we kids would try to catch a flying bat by hurling a cushion in the air, what a hope!! None of us were aware of the acute warning system that the bat has. The ability to receive sounds back from an object without being able to see it—a most incredible natural ability they have. Bats are not seen in the town's streets today. For instance, in Rose Street, there were six gas lamps—a very subdued light compared with the electric lights today. That must be the reason for their absence.

The children of the street had a variety of games that kept us amused for hours. One of the great pleasures was collecting and playing with cigarette cards. They are not available to youngsters today, but in my childhood every boy would walk around with a large pack of cards in his pocket secured by an elastic band. These would be used in a variety of ways, 'on tops', 'furthest', 'knock 'em down'—all quite self explanatory really. If you can't analyse it, ask any elderly gent in your community and he will know.

We had steel hoops with a skimmer—usually a butchers skewer with the end opened up to form a hook and the point inserted into a shaped piece of wood to form a handle.

'Whip and top'. We would travel up and down the street sending the top spinning away in front of us This was fine except on a wet day when the whip could so easily wrap itself around the top and send it flying through the air when we watched with bated breath in case it hit a window.

'Hide and seek', especially at dusk. There were lots of doorways and entrances where we would tuck ourselves away and await discovery. During the daylight hours the girls in the street would have skipping sessions—not just one girl with a rope. They would string a rope across the road and have a number of 'skippers' at the same time. Naturally they would be very upset if a vehicle came along and disturbed the routine. Can you imagine that scene today?

Of course during the season, 'conkers' would be all the rage challenges being issued in all directions and the unrealistic claims about this or that nut. "Mine`s a sixty-fourer", or whatever number came to mind. Then if you managed to break that conker, yours became a 'sixty-fiver'—harmless fun.

On many occasions, the Town Crier, Mr. Banks, would tour the town with a proclamation of some sort and I think he must have dreaded performing this duty in Rose Street. He would always be surrounded by the children of the street and, without fail, at the end when he shouted, "God save the King", there would be a united chorus of "What about the Queen?". This would occur three or four times as he moved along the street.

Characters abounded of course. At No.8, near the top of the road, lived a rather strange lady, Miss Feltham. Very few people in Rose Street, if any, knew what she looked like. On occasions she would be taken down the road to the church in a wheelchair pushed by a companion. She was always dressed in dark clothing with a shawl draped over her face and a hat that very much resembled a large lamp shade—a very mysterious figure. When she arrived at the church she would busy herself with cleaning, floral decoration or any job that needed to be done so she was clearly quite able—very odd.

At No.46 lived dear old Bertie Strange who, by all accounts, had a steel plate in his head following an injury in the 1914-18 war. With just a small amount of liquid refreshment he would be as happy as a lark, singing all the way home invariably followed by a couple of policemen who would position themselves opposite his house. He would stand on his doorstep, then he would walk to the edge of the path and call across to the constables, "You can catch me now!". As they moved across the road he would step back into his doorway and say, "You can`t catch me now!"—harmless and quite funny.

Another gentleman that liked his alcohol was Walt Neville. He lived at the rear of the Queens Arms but he invariably went into town for his refreshment, always dressed in a dark overcoat and a bowler hat. Facially he was almost the double of W.C. Fields, a film comedian of the past. On his way home he would scatter all his loose change across the road for the youngsters to scramble for—and they did.

It would take page after page to relate all the tales and memories about Rose Street but there was an occasion that is worth a mention. It revolves around Miss Gadd, the daughter of Isaiah. She lived at St. Mary's, No.26 Rose Street until a good age. She would host all sorts of events, mostly connected to the Wesleyan Chapel; in her very extensive garden. The Mothers' Union and other groups would be allowed to use the grounds for garden parties and such like. There was a very large garden swing which was always popular with the children of course.

This garden had a massive collection of apple trees and soft fruit bushes and one year Miss Gadd gathered a group of the children from the street together and asked us to pick her fruit. Thinking that this could be rewarding, we happily obliged. Having completed the task we were then let out through the front door and each given a paper bag containing a few windfall apples—not the reward expected. This same thing happened the following year and the mothers of the street were able to make fruit pies or jam or whatever they fancied from the proceeds handed over the back fence. Oddly we were never asked again.

The Hallworth premises.

I remarked earlier about the bakers, corn and grocery shop. This was at the bottom of the street—now in 2004, the premises of Wigmore's the removal company. The Hallworth family ran the bakers etc. and they also had a fine herd of cows which were grazed at the former Carnival Field or on Elms Field. These cattle were driven, usually by Billy Brooks and Ernie Milam, up Denmark Street, through the Market Place and down Rose Street for regular milking. The thing that we lads of the street found most upsetting was that not only did it disturb our game of football or cricket but after they had gone past, our ball would get very messy indeed. (This movement of cattle continued until the mid-1950s).

We were always able to play freely in the street because there was so little motorised traffic. The lorries from Talbot's coalyard would come in and out—'Colonel' Purver with his little bread van, and the milk van of Woodcray Manor. This was almost all there was. Most other deliveries were by horse and cart or pony and trap such as those of Knapps dairy from Embrook. The trap was driven by the cheeky chappie, Vic Challis who always wore a broad smile.

At one time our milk was delivered by a chap on a trade-bike with the churns in the front carrier. He would ladle the required amount from the churn into the milk jug. I recall on many occasions watching this operation. But the thing that always fascinated me was the fact that he would stop at the front step putting one foot on the step to balance to fill the jug. He always had a 'dew-drop' on the end of his nose and I recall watching that with some horror in case it dropped into our milk. Where were the Health and Safety people in those days?

Living in the first house of Queens Terrace was the Collier family of three brothers. One of them was a coal-man with the usual horse and cart. During the summer days he would cover the horse's ears to keep away the flies whilst the horse ate its bag of oats. This took place outside our frontage and mother used to speak about the horse's ear-caps with some humour. It was a long time before I grasped the fact that the 'ear-caps' were in fact a large pair of ladies brassieres.

25

Youngsters at Queen's Terrace

There was another occasion that involved the three brothers. When the chocolate laxative Ex-lax was introduced, many sample packets were put through people's letterboxes just to allow them to try the product. It appears that Bill, one of the three, decided that he was not going to share with his brothers so he ate the lot. At that time he was working on the new reservoir being constructed at Coppid Beech and, according to his workmates, he spent most of the day behind a hedgerow.

Rose Street itself has changed very little, and many of the properties are as they have been for very many years. Inevitably some have been demolished. The wall and buildings associated with the Heelas company, which included the mortuary near the top of the street, were situated more or less where W. J. Strange is now located. I know that, because, as a small boy, I always ran past the gateway just in case!!

The cottages that stood to the right of the Methodist Church and, of course, my former home to the left of the church, now parts of the church, occupy those sites. The row of cottages was named Queens Terrace. That was located where the roadway into the Marks & Spencer store now runs. A little further along was the coalyard of G. W. Talbot. This was followed by the cottages on the street front where there is now the wall of the M&S car park, and the Queens Arms public house, which stood in the entrance to Ash Court as it is today.

Where a massive change has taken place is behind the properties on the left from Wingmore Lodge down to Nos. 16-18 WADE Charity Shop. The gardens have been built over with the Waitrose Supermarket and there are other parts of the street where the rear areas have been developed either as buildings or car parks. I suppose that is progress.

At the bottom of the street there is new development on the site of the Tudor cottages that were demolished in 1938. With the development, the route of Cross Street has been changed for safety reasons. It is very noticeable how many cars leave Peach Street and travel up Rose Street, which is sad but inevitable. So many drivers feel the need to save as many seconds as they can.

For many years there were two well known delivery carts, pulled by some fine horses and driven by two local men. These were the delivery wagons of the railway. They would take heavy loads all around the town having loaded them from the goods trains down at the station. The two carters were Tom Phillips and Bob Hines and they were constantly moving goods around the town. Tom was a wholehearted supporter of Wokingham Town football team. He and his companions would stand at the bottom corner of the pitch giving full voice with their supporting shout of, "Come on Oakey!". I do know that I would not like to have been in a situation at that time to mention to them that the club had a Japanese founder and that they should be shouting, "Come on Satsumas!" This is the legend that is supposed to have been discovered in 2002/3, and I suspect that the many local gentlemen who set up the trust for the Finchampstead Road ground would no doubt be imitating spinning tops whilst lying in their graves.

A great favourite all around the town on a summer Sunday was 'Ice-cream Johnnie'. He was an Italian gentleman. As I recall, his name was Rossi or something similar. Anyway, he would travel the town on his motor-bike and side-car, which was a large cream box affair. He was always dressed in a brilliant white coat and wore a leather motor cycle helmet. In Rose Street one of his chosen spots was near the chapel, so it was very handy to pop out for the Sunday treat. A penny-worth of ice cream in a glass and a couple of wafers—delicious!! The mystery was, how did he keep the ice cream in such perfect condition? He travelled to Wokingham from Reading and spent the day in the town. How he achieved it, I don't know. I only know it was a great treat.

There was also the other ice-cream treat that many enjoyed any day of the week. The products of Walls and Eldorado—two companies that had men trundle around the streets with box tricycles selling wafers, cornets and fruit flavoured ice sticks. They were a great favourite of the youngsters and equivalent to today's ice-lollies. All were very acceptable but could not begin to compare with Ice-cream Johnnie's product.

Whilst on the subject of special treats, Easter was a time that children enjoyed and no doubt still do. There were Easter Eggs on the morning of Easter Day and my sister and I would go downstairs for breakfast filled with expectations. We were never let down. There was always a coloured boiled egg that had been cooked in one of the food colorants and accompanied by 'soldiers' to dip. The plate was always surrounded by a semi-circle of chocolate eggs in various sizes and designs—some just in brightly coloured foil and others in some form of cardboard carrier. The carrier would be in the shape of a train, a lorry or, in the case of my sister, it may have been a swan. I don't know if we were particularly lucky but all our aunts and uncles living locally bought us an egg and the same applied to our cousins. It was a ritual that we certainly enjoyed. With the coming of the war years, a drastic change came about—sweet rationing. We had enjoyed some wonderful times.

I mentioned early about the friendship that formed between my parents and Mr. and Mrs. Chapman. This lasted for very many years. One of the happy memories I have is of the Sunday evening walks, spring, summer and autumn. When weather permitted, the two families would meet, plus the two dogs. Both sides had a spaniel. Ours was named Don and the Chapman's was Mick. Both were from the same litter, and to watch the joy when they met was unbelievable.

We would set off across the meadows, usually taking the track where Norreys Avenue runs today, and take a path to a stile, which was opposite Warren House Road at its junction with Keephatch Road. Then walk to the Warren House (for some obscure reason, now called The Bullfinch) for a drink and a packet of crisps. Then walk along the Forest Road to a stile which gave access to the Ashridge meadows, now divided by the motorway. Then along Bell Foundry Lane to cross Bowyer's meadow—now all housing. Finally along Glebelands Road, Palmer School Road, Rose Court and home. Sometimes we would cover the same ground in the opposite direction. At that time this was a very pleasurable experience with so few cars to worry about. The birds, flowers, and berries were plentiful. It was simple but joyous pleasure.

All this was before the 1939-45 war. Life in the town at that time was so very different to today. In the Market Place lots of what we thought were exciting things happened, and the Carnivals were very special. The people of the town were so involved. Carnivals were invariably held on a Wednesday and at 8 o'clock in the morning a bugle would sound and the town began to buzz.

Wokingham Carnival stage.

Carnival Day. 'Guess the weight of coal' competition.
Young Ken in fancy dress stands guard.

Townsfolk dressed in all manner of costumes filled the streets. Those that wished to do so could collect a sealed box from the Town Hall and spend the day gathering pennies and half-pennies from the general public. Mostly this was in aid of the Wokingham Hospital.

Billy and Jimmy Brooks, plus one or two friends, with one of the group dressed as a very real life gorilla, would hire a barrel-organ and travel the streets jangling away. I recall being hoisted on to the lorry of Talbot's the coal merchants, where there was a huge piece of coal, and the public were asked to buy a ticket and guess the weight—the coal not me. The winner would have the equivalent amount of coal delivered to their home. I have wondered since how such a large piece of coal was brought up from the pit and delivered to Wokingham.

Lots of the shops and houses were decorated—some overall, but others just having a string of flags, but it all added to the gaiety of the day. The grand procession travelled around the town. It was always very spectacular with large floats, bands and pedestrians. All manner of things seemed to take ages to travel through the thronged streets and they would make their way to the Carnival

Field in Wellington Road where the lovely steam fair would be in full swing until at least midnight—what a day!

Competitions were arranged for decorated shops and also for decorated houses. This was something that father could not resist. He would spend hours up and down ladders decorating the house front in Rose Street. Another gentleman, who decorated his house more than most, was Mr. Bridgeman who lived at Elms Lodge at the bottom of Denmark Street. These two were always competing for the top accolade. Father invariably won first prize which pleased him greatly. The last time he did this was for the Coronation in 1953. I am just eternally grateful that the fashion for decorating with Christmas lights was not in vogue in his lifetime or the place would have been like Blackpool illuminations.

9 Rose Street decorated for Coronation.

The Carnivals that followed the 1939-45 war were to a great extent still big affairs. The processions at that time were made quite spectacular by the large companies that had moved into the area entering some very special floats. I well remember one that depicted an extremely large swan—obviously on a wire frame but the body was all white rosettes, probably made from crepe paper. On the carriage were some very attractive young ladies. Perhaps that is why I remember it so well.

There were many others equally spectacular. One very similar was a pink elephant. It may have been from another year by the same company, I cannot really remember. Somebody will put me right. I suppose that economics have now made this sort of thing impracticable in this area today.

Even at this period many townsfolk would dress in some fancy gear and walk around the town collecting. But there was one man who did not dress up, but rather undressed. He wore a grass skirt, carried a spear and was covered over all in black boot polish—a really fearsome looking warrior. It must have taken an age to get cleaned up, but the effect was certainly spectacular. I know who he was but feel I should let his family keep his anonimity.

For those that may make the connection, he was also a daredevil at the grass track racing at California after the closure of the former speedway meetings. At this time they rode ordinary motorcycles, and this chap would sit at the back of the field, then suddenly open the throttle and scatter all before him every which way, much to his own and the spectators delight. What a character!

Another event that took place in the Market Place was the animal sales with the cattle tied to the rails that ran along the Town Hall on the side opposite, where Smiths now stands. Not only the very strong rails, but at a point just to the left of the entrance to the present Information Centre, there was a weighing machine to weigh the cattle. This had been purchased by the council from the railway authorities at a cost of £10 and converted for its new use.

Alongside was a higher rail five to six feet high and some of the youngsters would perform all sorts of gymnastic feats on this bar despite the stone pavement below (see picture page 83).

Sheep and pigs were in the hurdle pens in the market area. Local farmers and also the butchers would be there to purchase some fine livestock, particularly the animals that had been decorated with a prize rosette. Perhaps they wished they had not won such a thing! A rather gory tale-piece to this story—Colebrook's invariably bought the prize bull and, as they had a slaughter-house at the rear of their premises, before evening the poor animal's head would be displayed in the shop front complete with all its prize rosettes.

In 1935, great celebrations took place in honour of the Silver Jubilee of King George V and Queen Mary. Although the population was much smaller than that of today, the town was heaving with people, and it was one of the events when all the school-children of the town received a commemorative mug.

Wokingham town centre now, and in recent years, has been the scene of the very popular Winter Carnival and the equally successful May Fair. In September the Town Hall is open to all and sundry with guided tours to all parts of the building and, in the afternoon, walks around the town. Members of the public have buildings, some of which have blue plaques placed by the Wokingham Society displayed on them, and other items of interest pointed out by members of the History Group.

Walkers gathering for guided town walk.

For very many years, crowds would gather on Boxing Day in the Market Place to witness the scene of the Garth Hunt gathering for the 'stirrup cup', the traditional drink supplied by a local hostelry.

They would move off into the countryside with a host of followers on foot or bicycles invariably down Wiltshire Road. The hunt would then set off across the meadows of Ashridge and beyond.

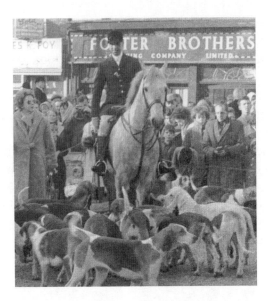

The Garth hunt in the Market Place.

The arrival of the motorway cutting across the hunting country as it did, meant an end to the Boxing Day Meet. The last Meet in the Market Place was on Boxing Day, 1961 and on 1st May, 1962. Garth Hunt amalgamated with South Berks Hunt and from then the Boxing Day Meet has been held at Ye Olde Turners Arms public house car park in Mortimer.

The regular events in the Market Place were, of course, the Friday and Saturday market days, when a variety of stalls would gather much as today. But the market day was much longer, whereas the market closes now by four o'clock. Pre-war people like Ben Messiah 'The Orange King' would come from Reading, set up his stall and have two very busy days.

On Saturday, many womenfolk would wait until quite late into the evening, bathed in the bright light from the lamps hanging from the stall. The lamps were probably a type of Tilley lamp, but they certainly lit the whole area. The reason for the ladies waiting so patiently was that Ben and his fellows would sell off the fruit at ridiculous prices. A large hand of bananas for sixpence (2p) and bags of oranges at give-away prices.

The Farmers' Market.

At the present time the Market is enjoying great success with the Farmers' Market held on the first Thursday of the month. The Market Superintendent, Colin Hook, has put in a great effort to bring farmers and other traders to Wokingham from many miles away. Two examples being a grower from Lincolnshire with fresh vegetables of excellent quality, at the right price, and fresh produce from Gray's Farm, the local growers, equally competitive.

There is so much more. Farmers with lamb, beef, pork, fresh trout, game, sea fish, and genuine free range eggs, plus lovely water cress from the Test Valley. Bakers with lovely pies, cakes, sponges and, of course, bread. The only problem, as far as the shoppers are concerned, is the amount of tempting products which leads to spending a lot of cash. Long may this event flourish.

There was for me, a very moving event very near to the Market Place. As far as I can recall it must have been about 1937. Mr. Eric Perkins had a cycle, radio and gramophone shop at No.1,

Denmark Street and, on this particular evening, he had a television set on demonstration in his shop window. Of course a large crowd had gathered to view this phenomenon. I, being a little whipper-snapper, managed to wriggle to the front and had my nose glued to the window thoroughly entranced by this miracle. How long I was there I have no idea but suddenly I was grabbed by the scruff of my collar and hauled back through the crowd by a very irate and worried mother.

As I said, it was a 'very moving event for me' being almost chased all the way home. It also demonstrated how we children in the town needed to behave. If the people around me had not known who I was, mother would not have found me. If any of us got into any sort of trouble, the news reached home before we did!

The Lee family of bakers moved into the adjoining shop to Mr. Perkins—a superb bakery—really delicious cakes. On Saturday evening it was not unusual to go to Lees and ask for a penny-worth of stale cakes. We would be given a few of these lovely cakes in a bag for our penny. They were never in any way stale, but could not be kept until Monday.

Youngsters today have fun on their skateboards or roller-blades—pieces of equipment never dreamed of when we were youngsters. We still had hours of enjoyment with strapped on roller-skates and the other great favourite, the trolley. We would scrounge a set of pram wheels and arrange them so that the front wheels would swivel, and fix them to a sturdy board. An orange box would then be mounted on this as a driving compartment, and with a rope attached each side of the front axle, we were able to steer and sail down slopes or hills with gay abandon. Speeding down Wiltshire Road from the bottom of Rose Street was a favourite run and, of course, the traffic situation again made all the difference. We never expected to meet a car.

Having remarked so emphatically about the lack of vehicles, it seems to me that my sister and myself did not appreciate how fortunate we were, because my father had an Austin Seven before the war. We enjoyed trips all over the south, often to the seaside but at least into the countryside to picnic. This was something that we had enjoyed for many years by travelling on bicycles to the woodlands at Ceasar's Camp near Crowthorne.

It was about this time that father purchased a basket side-car which could be attached to his bicycle. I have no idea where he found this, and it is the only one I have ever seen. What it did provide was hours of fun in the street. All the folk in the area tried to ride it but it either went round in circles or headed for the nearest lamp post. Eventually father gained the knack and was then able to carry Joyce in a very safe manner to our picnicking Sundays. From the pedal cycle and basket father progressed to a motor-bike and sidecar.

By this time we had discovered a wonderful picnic area behind a roadside screen of small silver birches—a large area of grassland and heather. We seemed to be the only people to visit there and we had quite a large family gathering at these events and spent many happy times. The area is well used today because it is the site of the Coral Reef swimming pool and its attendant fitness centre off the Nine Mile Ride.

Our picnic area.

37

Swimming party at Heathpool.

This same group of family and friends also enjoyed swimming at Kingsmere or Heathpool when both lakes were free to use and certainly in a much cleaner state than today.

On one occasion Peter Hare, a close friend, and I were sitting on the sandy bank alongside Kingsmere on the Nine Mile Ride—now fenced and with a hedgerow. We had a bottle of drink with us but no food. Along came one of the Walls ice-cream salesmen so we were able to spend the one penny we had between us to purchase a packet of wafers—not a feast but better than nothing.

On another occasion we had cycled along what at that time was a silver sandy track—Hollybush Ride to Heathpool. On arrival I realised that I had forgotten my swimming trunks. Not to be outdone Peter stripped and dived in after which he slipped off his trunks and handed them to me so that I could follow suit. We left the water in the same way by making the swap.

With the onset of war things became quite difficult for the private motorist with petrol rationing curtailing the use of the car. Many folk just put their vehicles up on blocks for the duration, but there was a reward because vehicles that had cost very little pre-war became very valuable assets after the war with no new cars available.

As a boy, I also enjoyed many other motorised trips, probably more than most of my contemporaries. My father spent most of his working life as a butcher. He became a butcher's shopman with S. A. Pither in Broad Street—now the premises of the Newbury Building Society. On Saturdays he would load the small blue van with the orders to be delivered to many of the large houses around the area. I presume to have some company, he would take me with him. So very early on in my young life I saw much of the local countryside.

Another highlight I remember came about because Mr. Pither had purchased a brand new Ford saloon, probably in 1937. Mrs. Pither wished to visit relations living in Epsom, Surrey. Either Mr. Pither had no wish to drive there, or did not want to visit his in-laws. So he asked Dad to take Mrs. Pither on the Sunday and saying that he could also take the rest of our family with him. This was eagerly accepted and off we went in this brand new car.

Mother was never at a loss when a picnic hove in view, so we were well prepared. Having dropped off Mrs. Pither, we drove to Epsom Racecourse to enjoy the food. Obviously this was too good an opportunity to miss, so we walked round the racecourse, and I galloped around Tattenham Corner probably thinking I was Gordon Richards.

Some wonderful outings could be had by booking on Herring's Coaches, or Benham's Coaches, based in Peach Street. They were not called coaches at that time but 'char-a-bancs'. A canvas roof that could be rolled back, not very luxurious seating, and how long those journeys to the coast took I hate to think. These same coaches were used on the occasion of 'Beating the Bounds' when organised parties travelled around the Borough boundary. There was much jollity as people were either made to lay across the boundary stone and receive a playful spank with a birch, or be lifted bodily and gently bumped on the boundary stone. Who would do that today?

Later, of course, we had more luxurious travel in the coaches of Brimblecombe Bros, at Eddystone Garage in Finchampstead Road sited where the garage is now between the two railway bridges, by the standards of that time they were wonderful.

Coach outing to Southsea. My family at front right. The Chapman's are standing behind.

Beating the Bounds.

Charles Marks and William T. Martin bumping Egerton Thorpe,

All this was summer activity. Now I am not totally convinced about global warming, but it does seem that we do not get the very severe winter weather in this region that occurred on occasions in the past. About 1934-5 the Kingsmere lake froze so solidly that one fellow had a brazier on the ice and was selling roasted chestnuts. I also clearly remember watching a young man on ice skates, who was extremely proficient, racing around the lake whilst many others did their best to stay upright. There were no rinks in the area for people to learn the skill.

A few years later a number of us boys from Palmer School made our way to the frozen pond near Ludgrove School (Wixenford School). We searched amongst the trees to find something suitable to use as a hockey stick. Then using a flat stone as a 'puck', we proceeded to slide all over the place having a very hectic game. We were brought to an abrupt halt when Arthur Paice, who lived in 'the overhangs', crashed to the ice and lay very still with a lump the size of a duck's egg formed on his forehead. We gathered round quite convinced that Arthur had suffered severe injury if not death. To our great relief he finally stirred and slowly regained his senses. We all left the scene and wandered home in a very quiet mood.

Many years later, Wokingham was buried beneath a very heavy snow-fall. The problem then was that it would not melt. The weather stayed very cold for weeks and the piled up snow became dirtier and dirtier. Finally it was shovelled on to lorries and deposited on the Carnival Field and there it finally melted away.

Just a few years ago I awoke one Sunday morning to see a landscape glistening white with hoar-frost. I dressed very quickly and grabbed the camera, walking swiftly across Langborough Recreation Ground and on to the Ludgrove area, taking dozens of pictures as I went. I had never witnessed such a wonderful scene before nor since. These pictures formed a slide show named 'A Winter's Morn' that has been appreciated at many club meetings around the area.

Returning to my boyhood period, horses played such a vital part of life in the 1930s. A great event locally was the Point-to-Point held over the fields of Ashridge and Norreys. Mostly the riders were farmers riding the horses that they used for hunting, and they would ride the course over some very high jumps. Sadly, some came to grief and quite often their mounts suffered broken legs. They were humanely destroyed on the spot. The distraught rider, who was often the owner, would be led away from the scene by friends.

But for all that sadness it was always a great occasion and it was not unusual for the Prince of Wales, later Edward VIII, and later still, Duke of Windsor, to participate in this spectacular event.

On one such occasion, I recall being in the field where the houses are on the left of Norreys Avenue down to Coronation Square. In this field there were some large carts placed either side of the finishing line where the judges were stationed—no chance of photo-finishes then. These same carts were used when there was an occasion to have a school outing, when we would be taken to meadow land near the town for a trip 'in the country'. Today's children expect at least a journey to Europe for the school trip.

Ascot Race week was another 'horsey' occasion that had quite an effect on the town before the war, much more so than today. The two great joys for the children of the town at that time was taking car numbers of the vehicles travelling to the races, and later in the day, to cheer the coaches on their way home. These all travelled through the town on their way to places west of us. We children had our favourite spots. We would cheer like mad as each coach passed by and the occupants threw coppers from the windows. It then depended upon how quick we were to beat our rivals to gather them up.

On reflection, I am not too sure why I bothered with this activity, because Ascot Week was a very lucrative time for me. Having a fair amount of space at home, Mother had a regular group of 'bookies' who came for bed and breakfast at the time of the meeting. One of them would hand me a florin (10p), or half-crown (12p), to run up to town for a newspaper. On my return the usual comment was, "keep the change son!"—and it may have happened two or three times each morning. I was a willing errand boy—riches beyond belief.

A few years later, I was doing an hour long paper round six days a week for 3/6d (17p). Money seemed to be no object to these fellows. I remember an occasion when one of them went into town to purchase a 'straw boater' to wear at the course. As he entered the gate at home one of his friends took it off his head and kicked it across the yard. There followed a furious few seconds of football and the yard was covered with pieces of straw.

Well into the 1940s the Rose Inn was a residential hotel, and before the war it was a wonderful sight to see the ladies and gents in their finery boarding the horse drawn carriages to travel to Ascot. The race week certainly had a great effect on the town.

In the 1930s a flying club would visit the town to give flights over the area for a very reasonable fee. Just taking one or maybe two people at a time, they would take off from Frog Hall Green, the official name of the field, although we locals always called it 'the Plannie'. It is now the site of St. Crispin's School. What a wonderful experience that must have been at that time to be able to fly over the town. Sadly, like all the other children, I was too young.

The fields and meadows around the town were our other playgrounds. Many would cross over Langborough Recreation Ground across to the Bell, the stream that runs across from what is now called Ludgrove it used to be Wixenford, and travels across the fields to Finchampstead Road and then on until it joins or becomes the Emmbrook.

On the other side of town were the meadows that have been submerged under the housing estate of Norreys. This was particularly the favoured area of the boys from Rose Street where we would fashion bows and arrows and spend the whole day being Robin Hood or whoever was the flavour of the month—wonderful carefree days.

These are the memories that folk have when they will tell you that it was always long sunny days in the summer. It was not the case of course, as the Met. Office records will show. It was very much as today. Anyway, we would go off with probably a bottle of home-made lemonade, made up with the yellow powder and water, and maybe a sandwich.

It is a sad thought that today's youngsters do not enjoy that style of life, but we live in an ever changing world. One small bonus from the area—eggs, farm chickens would really be 'free range', and it was not too unusual to find an egg or two that had been laid in the hedgerows. Without doubt they should have been taken to the farm but children do not think like that.

Most of the heroes we would mimic were the film heroes that we had viewed on screen at the Savoy, which sometimes went under the other name of the 'Bug-house'. They did have some cracking adventure films. We would pay three-pence (between one and two pence in today's money) and have a wonderful afternoon on Saturday. There was a door to the right of the screen which was an exit also leading to the toilets. Going out that way, and along what is now called Broad Street Walk, we would go home for tea. If it had been a particularly good programme, it was simple to return by the same route and see it all over again. What little rogues we were!!

The Savoy was lit by gaslights and the walls were decorated with some wonderful jungle scenes of monkeys swinging in the trees and other jungle images. All these were painted by a very talented man—Mr. Dick Giles, the local sign writer.

The Commissionaire was Mr. Horace Blake, a stern former army man who had spent many years in the service. He was ram-rod straight and sported a fine waxed moustache with twirled ends—quite a character.

Sometime after the Ritz Cinema opened in 1937, he was transferred to perform the same role there. He lived with his Indian born wife at 'Sobraon Place', Cockpit Path. Also living there was his daughter Dorothy, and in the days of the silent movies at the Savoy, Dorothy would play the dramatic music to accompany the film.

Living next door was my grandmother, aunt and uncle and family. Gran was Mrs. Louise Case, and Aunt and Uncle were Moses and Emily Dance and their three children, Ernest, William and Sheila. Also living there was one of the town's finest darts players, Hubert Case.

The site of this pair of houses is now a jungle of brambles etc. at the bottom of Howard Road, so different to the Howard Road that

I knew as a boy. Facing up the road, on the left, were Sales' trial grounds filled with beds of plants, plus a lovely walnut tree—all enclosed by a yew hedgerow and chestnut fencing.

During the war this area was taken over for the British Restaurant—a place to obtain a reasonably priced meal. There were a number of these opened during the war. It later became the Waterloo Restaurant owned by Mr. Ifould. On the right was Sales' orchard, now the premises of the Sales Memorial homes—nice bungalows for some of the towns elderly residents. Change is inevitable, but I have to say it grieves me to see the area where Sobraon Place once so proudly stood now just wasteland.

Equally sad was the demolition of 'Hobart Place'—a row of five nice houses at the bottom of Cockpit Path which were demolished to make way for the inner distribution road which, of course, never came into being. These houses were built by the father figure of the Perkins family who had lived in Hobart, Tasmania. On coming home he had this block built probably as an investment. They were numbered 1-5 from the bottom upwards and in No.5 lived another aunt and uncle—Cecil and Elsie Case and two cousins, Beryl and Joan. All this location is now car park.

Whilst in this area let us take a look at the top end of Cockpit Path, walking from Red Lion passage across the car park to the entrance to Palmer Gardens. This had been for a long time the route from Cockpit Path to a bowling green. The gardens were for many years the site of the Howard Palmer Bowling Green which was reputed to be one of the finest in the county, and certainly county matches were often played there. I know that we children would scramble up the fence in Luckley Path to watch the bowls but not really understanding the game.

If you can picture the path across the car park. To the left of the path were Gladstone Cottages, a pair of semi-detached houses that for some years had been the homes of the Beasley family and the Milam family—all local people. Then one of them became the home of another branch of my family—Aunt and Uncle, Bert and Ada Hutt, and their children, Cyril, Vera and twins, Rene and Gwen, Ronald and Dennis. It is pleasing to know that many members of these families still live in the town today.

Returning to the Cockpit Path area, just a little higher towards Sturges Road and opposite the Salvation Army Hall stood two small timber framed cottages. At the far end of these were the stables where the Co-operative Society stabled the horses that pulled the bakery delivery carts. At the time I remember, the folk living there were the Marriners and the Loaders. In place of these picturesque cottages, we now have re-cycling bins of various colours—not quite so nice to look at.

Having close family ties in the Howard Road area I naturally spent a good deal of time there, and the family Christmases were always held 'round home', which was where Gran lived—happy days!

On reflection, I realise that in fact they could have been quite tragic days. My uncle had a passion for decorating at Christmas. Paper chains festooned from every part of the ceiling and in a corner by the fireplace always stood a fine natural Christmas tree reaching from floor to ceiling. Presents were piled at the foot and the tree was dressed with many, many baubles and dozens of candles in little clip-on holders. The electric lights of today could not be used in many houses with only a gas supply.

With the room filled with boisterous children and partying adults I dread to think what might have happened if just one of those candles had ignited any part of the tree. In moments it would have been a blazing inferno, it so easily might not have been 'Happy days'.

Very early in my school days, Mr. W.T. Martin had built, and eventually opened to the public, a very fine swimming pool complete with diving boards, a chute, fountains and children's paddling pool. The entrance to his grounds was off the Milton Road. This was a delightful haven in the town enjoyed by everyone that went there either to swim or just laze and picnic on the lovely lawns.

On some very chilly mornings we would be taken from Palmer School to have swimming lessons. These sessions actually began in June, 1937. This is an activity that has never been close to my heart, even in warm weather. Although having said that, Peter and

46

myself would visit the pool early on a Sunday morning when the gardener was sweeping the leaves and litter and have a free dip. But it was more than a little cool at times. When we visited with the school I distinctly remember that another of my school pals was a great swimmer. Gordon Norcutt would swim fifty lengths whilst the rest of us were threshing around.

Martin's Pool.

I really do believe that I have been blessed with a very good memory, because I clearly recall my mother and father taking me round the gardens of Mr. Martin before the pool was built. I can only have been a very small child at that time, but I can still see the heather beds and gravel paths. Martin's Pool is no more of course. The site now has houses in a group known as Poppy Place.

During my school years, many changes took place. In the mid thirties the first major development of Peach Street took place when the town houses, low shops and some small properties were demolished. They were replaced by the block of shops where Woolworth's still occupy their original position.

In the early days of the store, it was an entirely different place. Along the right hand side there was a tea bar that we would visit during the mid-morning break, for a cuppa and ham roll—very enjoyable. The counters were parallel with a walkway between where the young ladies would serve the customers. There was no self service at that time.

When the store was first opened it was still boasting to be the 3d. and 6d. Store. If, for instance, one wished to purchase a tea set comprising six plates, six cups, six saucers and a teapot, the cost would be 6d. per plate, 6d. per saucer, 6d. for the teapot and 6d. for the teapot lid—a total of 10/-. Now I am aware that this is all nonsense to the younger generations. In fact it amounted to 50p, in today's terms. But it must be realised that 50p was a great deal of money to many people at that time—almost a week's wages to cleaning ladies and the like.

In all that row of shops Woolworth's is the only business that has remained constant. All the other premises have changed hands at various times. At the time of this development, a young man came from Herne Bay in Kent to install the counters in the new Woolworth premises. He must have learned that mother sometimes gave accommodation to lodgers and he called at No.9 and, at the time, he was welcomed to stay for the duration of the job. In the event he stayed with us for some years, and Jack eventually married a local girl, and they raised a family.

About the same period, another very important development was the building and opening of the Ritz cinema in 1937. This was quite a palatial building, much superior to our old favourite, the Savoy. The seats were plush and very comfortable. There were the stalls and the circle, all approached over thick carpeting.

However there was one great error of judgement with this fine building. It seems that the surveyors had not taken into consideration the fact that they were building on an area that had rather a lot of sawdust in the ground. This had been part of a timber yard. Anyway, they decided to line the foyer with mirrors from floor to ceiling. It looked fantastic, but in a very short period of time, the building subsided only a little but it was enough to crack the mirrors from top to bottom. It was then that the normal style of decorative plaster work was put in place. The Ritz was closed some years ago and a bingo hall developed on the site in Easthampstead Road.

Despite the fact that this fine cinema had only just opened, the planners decided in 1938 to demolish the fifteenth century cottages at the bottom of Rose Street, which in earlier times had been the homes of some of the town's silk knitters. This was to allow the building of another cinema. An amazing decision to make, in view of the fact that Rose Street is one of the finest medieval streets in the country. Once the cottages were empty, the children had a new adventure playground. It must have been quite dangerous, but also a great temptation. I have to admit to being one of the young vandals involved in that. With the outbreak of war in 1939, the cinema plan was scrapped.

Tudor Cottages, Rose St. demolished in 1938.

In 1938, the Wokingham Town Football Club arranged the opening of a new stand opposite to the shed-like arrangement on the other side of the pitch. Of course an event like this demanded something rather special, so Chelsea F.C. were invited to play a match against the town team. I watched the game from behind the goal at the Finchampstead Road end. Keeping goal for Chelsea in the second half was John Jackson, the Scottish international keeper. At the final whistle I dived under the rope, programme in hand, to get his signature. Just as I got to him the National Anthem began and so I had a few moments conversation with this top class player.

As I mentioned earlier, the nickname of the team with the spectators—and there were quite a number—was Oakey. They would shout, "Come on Oakey!". The name was derived from the oak tree connection with Wokingham, and also the fact that for a spell Wokingham was named Oakingham. It is pleasing to note that the roadway on the housing estate, built on the former football ground, has been named Oakey Drive, thus perpetuating the well known and favoured name.

Dr. Ernest Smith, President of the Football Club opening the stand.

The other three gentlemen, from left to right: Jack Langley, Harold Lee and David Goddard.

oOo

The War Years, 1939 – 1945.

With the outbreak of the war with the Axis alliance of Germany and Italy in 1939, Wokingham was one of the selected areas to become the home for evacuees from London and Kent. Some of these folk arrived as families—mother and children, but many children were taken from their homes, for their own safety, to comparative quiet areas like Wokingham. This must have been a most traumatic situation for these children. Taken around the streets of a strange town and being handed over to a family they had never met, and left to make their home with them.

At 9 Rose Street, a nervous young girl was left with us by the Evacuation Officer. Her name was Margery. She had travelled from her home in Welling, Kent, separated from her friends, and left in the home of a family of whom she had no knowledge. It is difficult to imagine the feelings that this child must have had. I know that, at the time, I gave it very little thought. On reflection, so many years later, I can visualise how awful that must have been.

Anyway, Margery soon settled down and we became very firm friends. It was at this time, coincidentally, that my sister Joyce was deemed to have a medical condition that entailed her being hospitalised for quite a long period. So I suppose that Margery became almost a substitute sister to me. Fortunately Joyce returned home fit and well and, when things became quieter, Margery's family took her home again. I still correspond with Margery to this day.

There were very many evacuees in the area and this did cause some disruption to our schooling. The recognised schools were used half day by the local children and half by the evacuees. At Palmer School, the children of St. Agnes C. of E. School, Kennington, were given lessons in the afternoon.

Whether it was fact or imagination, I am not sure. We locals felt that while they were using our classrooms, they were not treating the desks and books with the same respect that we ourselves did. It was probably a fanciful idea.

Many of the evacuated children were schooled in other premises. The schoolroom in Milton Road was one such location—now Martin & Pole salerooms. Virtually any sizeable place that could accommodate a class was pressed into service. Many of the children and families returned home after quite a short period, but I know that some remained and settled down in Wokingham. So perhaps they were not that unhappy.

We were very fortunate in Wokingham. Damage to property was fairly minimal, but the population were sometimes a little disturbed by some bombs in the area. Being frightened did not constitute being injured, fortunately.

There were one or two funny little episodes, like the time that a 'doodlebug' engine stopped over the town. We all knew that when that happened, it was due to come down. Everyone took shelter, but the flying bomb travelled on to land in an area of Emmbrook, causing no damage or loss of life.

On another occasion, early in the war, and after the evacuees had arrived, the air-raid siren went. The family took shelter in the very strong cellar under the house. We then realised that Margery was not with us and I dashed back up to see where she was, only to find her on a very dark stairway groping around for her 'gobstopper'—a large round sweet which she had dropped. These were a great favourite with children at that time.

This cellar in which we took shelter was, of course, the original beer cellar where the crates and barrels would have been lowered by the draymen. One great advantage was the water supply that was available. As with so many properties in Wokingham, there was an underground stream. In the cellar was a small arch, a receptacle could be lowered into the well and water drawn up. Dad had this water analysed by the chemist at the Berks Pharmacy and it proved to be very pure drinking water. We never had a need to use it. However, it was there if an emergency arose.

The nearest thing to a real disaster was when a large explosive— some say an aerial torpedo—landed in the Plannie. This was the meadow where St. Crispin's School is today. Had it landed on the houses just across the road, it would have been devastating.

Even that event had a touch of humour. All the tiles and slates of the houses stood up like rows of soldiers where the blast went under them. Of course, all the windows were shattered, which was not so funny, but happily the occupants all survived.

There were other cases of near devastation—a large bomb in the garden of a house near the present day Guide Dog Centre. The aforementioned doodlebug landed at Emmbrook, fortunately missing the houses. There were numerous small bombs and incendiaries in the area, but life and limb survived. Considering everything, Wokingham was a lucky place to be. Sadly, a number of young people serving in the forces lost their lives, or came home with severe injuries— the inevitability of war.

The local people of the town, who had not been called up to the armed forces, probably had the hardest task of all. They were the local firemen who had been given the title of National Fire Service. These men, all volunteers, spent many long and dangerous hours during the blitz, travelling to London and returning the next day. Most of them had a business to run. It really must have been a thankless task.

Wokingham Fire Brigade during the war.

There was one occasion when they had a light hearted interlude. A house in Cross Street, formerly the home of Mr and Mrs Swadling, was to be demolished. In order to give the firemen a little practice, it was decided to set fire to the property. The crews took up station in front and behind the house, watched by a large crowd. These fellows, however, were out for fun and they spent more time playing the hoses over the house, dousing each other and, sometimes, a too close spectator, than they did on the fire. They really enjoyed it.

Another voluntary force was of course, the LDV Local Defence Volunteers, nicknamed 'Look, Duck and Vanish'. The first group was formed up in the Market Place with their armbands and broomsticks. Things changed rather rapidly when they were re-named the Home Guard and issued with Lee Enfield rifles, plus bayonets. They were ready to defend to the death if need be. They may have seemed rather like Dad's Army, but there was no doubting their intent.

Frank Perkins leads the Home Guard in their 'standing down' parade.

One of the commanding officers in the Home Guard was Mr. Frank Perkins, a member of the family who owned the garage at the top of Broad Street. Not only did he serve in that capacity, but he also spent many hours laboriously documenting the service of

Wokingham men and women, which branch of the services where they served and if killed, wounded or captured. It is a truly remarkable piece of work, which, I believe, is now stored at the Berkshire Record Office. Added to that, he also organised the production and distribution of leather wallets, with the town crest and the recipient's initials in gold. These were presented at the end of hostilities. I still have mine.

Many of the civilian population were called upon to perform various duties. The air raid wardens kept a constant watch on the streets to detect any stray light that may be issuing from any doorway or window. The cry, "Put that light out!", was not uncommon. Many young men and women were called upon to do duty as plane spotters and fire watchers—often a cold and lonely job.

Life in the town was much changed by the forces of the USA and Canada, plus troops from the Netherlands, being housed in the town—much to the delight of some residents, but much against the grain for others. They were very free with their gifts and, of course, the children loved the amount of chewing gum being tossed around. These troops spent a lot of time and money at the fairground, which seemed to be an almost permanent feature on the waste land in Cross Street. Although they were billeted here for some time and became a regular sight around the town, almost overnight they vanished.

'D' Day was imminent and the town resounded for many hours to the noise of tanks and other heavy vehicles making their way to the coast carrying troops of all the army units in the area. Many units marched from the town, probably to the station. It was an incredible sight. I do not believe the residents of Wokingham realised how many troops were in the close vicinity of the town.

During the war years, the great slogan, as I mentioned earlier, had been 'Dig for Victory' and my Dad had always had an allotment in the Ashridge plots. He continued to work that until he was called up to join the RAF. He used to take me with him to the allotment site and I would carry water, push seed potatoes into holes and do all sorts of mundane jobs. In truth, I became very disenchanted with the gardening scene and, I am afraid, that has remained with me to this day.

In the latter part of 1939, I became a newspaper delivery boy for Mr. Harold Lee in Peach Street. This also had a magic moment when, early one morning, the air raid siren sounded and one of the lads came tearing along on his bike wearing his gas mask. He was taking no chances. There were many problems with newspapers at that time. Often they would arrive at the shop much too late for the boys to get the rounds together and do deliveries before school. We would get as far as we could, hurry to school, then finish the deliveries during the school dinner time, often to the annoyance of our mothers. This was my introduction to Mr. Harold Lee. It was the beginning of a very long working association.

It is my belief that most of us felt that the mothers of this country had one of the most difficult tasks during the war years, having to feed the family members with such frugal rations. The amounts allowed are difficult to imagine, but just try to visualise the situation. Rationing actually came into force on the 8th January, 1940, four months after war started. The allowance per person was

2oz.(56.25g) butter
4oz (113.4g) margarine, alternating weekly
2oz (56.25g) lard
2oz.(56.25g) cheese
4oz.(113.4g) bacon
3.5oz (99.3g) cooked bacon or ham
1 egg
2ozs (56.25g) tea
1lb. (453g) sugar per month.

Dried fruit, raisins, sultanas etc. were also rationed. Tinned fruit and salmon etc. were virtually unobtainable.

These were some of the items for a week per person. Just weigh these amounts and get an idea of the problem. It is certain that many mothers were self sacrificing to feed their families.

Meat rationing came into force on the 14th March, 1940. Offal (liver, kidneys, hearts etc.) was free of rationing. As soon as any of

56

these things became available, the housewives would gather like bees round a honey-pot and the supply went in minutes.

Imported fruits, like bananas and oranges, became non-existent. Sweets of any sort were on ration and the children, who were sweet lovers, would barter in every possible way to get extra coupons. Eventually clothing was rationed. Ration books were issued for all these goods and a strict control was maintained.

To help eke out the meat situation, Peter and I did a little rabbitting around the countryside, and we also bred rabbits for the table. I have to say, I always regretted having to kill these animals, but that was the purpose of the exercise. Rationing of many items continued into the early years of the 1950s.

Housewives had additional problems to deal with. Running and maintaining a home in those times was very hard and laborious work. Take clothes washing as an instance. The copper had to be lit with wood and kept fuelled while in use. This was often a brick built corner piece, with a metal liner, in which the clothes had to be boiled, scrubbed clean on the scrubbing board. They were then put through the very heavy mangle to take out excess water, hung on the clothes line to dry and, finally, ironed with flat irons that had to be heated on the kitchen range, or gas ring. Two irons were used in rotation. As one cooled off, it was changed for the heated one.

Also, it must be realised that the materials were very different to today. Sheets were of heavy linen, or even flannelette. Husbands doing their normal work, such as my father, wore white smocks and aprons in the butcher's shop. All these items were washed at home, whereas today, the company will almost certainly have all staff clothing laundered. It sounds like pure drudgery, and it was.

The remaining household tasks were no less arduous. Today, bed-making is a simple task, with duvets and well upholstered mattresses of various types—making it very easy.

Before the advent of these luxuries, it was an entirely different story. Housewives dealt with flock mattresses. These would become very lumpy and they had to shake and pummel them to try to get a reasonably even surface—a heavy task. In many homes, they had the additional chore of chamber pots. Outside toilets were the norm at lots of homes. The 'jerry' under the bed for relief during the night was a must. These had to be emptied and rinsed every morning. Not the most pleasant task of the day. I sometimes wonder how these dear ladies maintained their sanity.

All housework was very heavy going because there were none of the labour saving devices of today. Elbow grease and determination were the order of the day. How times have changed and I am sure will change again over the next fifty years.

Whilst thinking of changes over the years, in the 1930s and 40s the radio was the main source of entertainment in the home, plus the gramophone. The radio in most homes ran on batteries, plus an accumulator, which could be charged at the local garages etc. This involved an electric charge being delivered into the acid at a cost to the customer of 6d. (2½ pence). The large battery and the small grid-bias battery were dry and it was inevitable that if a major event, such as a heavyweight boxing match from America, was being broadcast late at night, one or other of the batteries would 'die'— very frustrating!!

The changes in television have been absolutely amazing. The sets, just after the war, were mostly large pieces of furniture with a small 9" (32cm) screen. Enclosed in the large cabinet was a mass of wires and valves, plus a lot of empty space. But the cabinet looked impressive. For years there was talk of coloured television, but this seemed a pipe-dream. Today, of course, it is accepted without question. I am always astounded to be able to view events in full colour from all over the world, as they happen.

Another great change that has taken place over many years—bed warming. At one time the upper classes would have used a warming pan, which was a brass or copper pan attached to a long handle. This pan was a closed unit. That is to say—a bottom and lid. This would be filled with hot coals or ashes and moved over the bed surface by a servant in preparation for the master and mistress to retire. Lesser beings would warm the bed with an ordinary house brick, put in the oven, and then transferred to the bed—quite efficient.

During my early years, we had hot water bottles—not the nice covered cuddly ones of today. They were either stone or metal and were they hot—especially the metal ones. It was always necessary to cover them with some material to make them tolerable. Today, of course, many people have an electric blanket to give them a warm welcome. It demonstrates the sort of advances that have been made in quite a short time.

oOo

The Youthful Years

At the age of fourteen, I left Palmer School to take up full employment with Harold Lee. I had worked for him as a newsboy and, on some Saturday mornings, I had been into the printing works to watch over one of the machines that had been set running.

I had become quite interested and, just prior to my leaving school, Mr. Lee asked me if I would like to take a job in the print works. This I happily did. This was my employment for the next fifty one years, plus part time for another five years. I never applied for a job and only ever had the one. That is, except for my period of three years army service—February 1945 to February 1948, which I did not happily do. Although, I suppose, it was an experience that should not have been missed. Two years of that time was spent in Germany, but that is getting beyond my youth.

My early years at work were, at times, very difficult. The male staff had all been called to the armed forces, except Mr. Lee, who was exempt, as all men running a single handed business were entitled to be. Cyril Crookson, who lived with Mr. and Mrs. Lee, was working away all day on munitions and, in the evening, operated the 'Intertype' to set type for various jobs.

One of the most important jobs, at that time, was the Wokingham Rural District Council minutes for all the various committees. As is the nature with such things, they were always a last minute rush, especially with the limited staff. They would come in at very short notice and had to be delivered by 4 o'clock on the last Friday of the month. Even at the age of fourteen, I sometimes worked until late evening and started again at perhaps 6 o'clock the next day. One needed to be very conscientious to operate in that way. I suspect that not too many of the youth of today would be prepared to do that.

Apart from the printing works, Mr. Lee had another great interest. He was a keen rabbit breeder—and I am talking about

National Champion class rabbits. His main interest was in the Chinchilla breed and he would send the animals by train to all parts of the country to participate in the shows. One of his great champions had a fancy show name, but at home, he was always referred to as 'Skipper'. Owners would send their does—again from all over the country, to mate with Skipper. Mr. Lee was also responsible for introducing the Lynx Rex breed to this country—a beautiful light tanned breed with a very short silky coat. Again, he had great success with this species in shows.

We had a trade bike with a very low slung carrier on the front— ideal for carrying the transport boxes for the rabbits. I would take them down to the station and pay for their carriage and, of course, on their return, I would take the bike down to the station to collect them.

On one occasion when I was due to collect, I could not find the bike. We searched high and low, eventually deciding that I would have to walk down and carry them back. So off I went and when I got to the station (the old original Victorian building), propped against the wall, was the bike where I had left it two days before!!

Mr. Lee would suddenly make up his mind to do something other than printing. On one occasion, out of the blue, he said, "Come on cocker. We are going to a sale". With that it was into the car and off we went to Holme Grange. This had been the home of The Hon. Mrs. Weston, and Messrs. Watts & Son were holding an auction to sell off the contents of the house.

This was a whole new experience to me. I had never been to an auction sale before. I believe I must have stood like a statue in case I bought something I didn't want and certainly could not afford. I did find it an interesting experience and I recall that Mr. Lee purchased a Grandfather clock—a very nice piece.

Holme Grange became a school soon after that and one of the early headmasters was Mr. John Graves, a brother of Robert Graves, the world renowned poet. John Graves would often come into the print works to order work to be done. He was a kindly man.

In 1944, we had an addition to the family—a brother to Joyce and myself. Graham was a really bonny baby and his early period showed great promise. What we did not know at that time was that he had the muscle wasting disease, muscular distrophy.

This, of course, was a tremendous blow to the whole family. Graham had a very positive attitude to life, coupled with the fact that he possessed a fine brain. He was involved in all sorts of activities in the town, but his one great love was the Wokingham Theatre. He was capable of producing and directing plays, but his great interest was aiding and encouraging the young members of the group.

He was also a member of the Wokingham Colorphoto Society. He had a specially adapted camera holder fixed to his wheelchair and, in fact, he produced some very good work with the camera.

He produced an audiovisual show called, 'The changing face of a town'. This demonstrated the development of the housing estates in Wokingham and other areas of modernisation. He also had a talent for artistic work, particularly with scraper board images of animals etc. He was becoming less able to do all these things and he died very suddenly at the age of thirty three years, having enjoyed an interesting and productive life.

But back to our teenage leisure time, which was spent in various ways. Youth clubs were very popular, and it was quite a simple matter to become a member of the chosen group. The Wokingham Junior Sports & Social Club was very popular. This club was run by Mr. David Goddard, a gentleman that gave much to the town. He was a Borough Councillor and, in fact, became Mayor, and an Alderman.

The youth club gave us the opportunity to take part in a variety of sports—football, tennis, and many indoor activities, such as table tennis, billiards, darts etc. Being a member of such an association gave one a sense of responsibility and a pride of being part of the town's community.

There was also The Wokingham Youth Club that offered the opportunity to learn ballroom dancing. This took place in the Town Hall at the time when it was permissible to dance in that lovely hall. We were taught, or attempted to be taught, by a very patient lady, who, over many years, has also put so much caring into her life. At the time of the youth club she was Miss Diana Molloy. Today, she is so very well known as Mrs. Diana Brimblecombe, taking pity on, and caring for hundreds of stray and unwanted animals.

Dances in the Town Hall, at that time, were quite a feature of Saturday nights. There was also dancing in the Drill Hall in Denmark Street—yes, we did once have a hall in Wokingham. Many lads and lasses would get on their bikes and ride to California to dance in the marvellous ballroom there. Apart from the Saturday night hops, there were occasions when a Grand Ball would be organised and these were quite magnificent affairs. I suspect that these sort of activities for the less affluent members of society have been priced out of reach today.

Another activity, from which we derived much pleasure, was the theatre. On Saturdays, Peter and I would purchase an Evening News newspaper to keep us occupied on the bus, mainly by reading the chosen week-end ramble by 'Fieldfare', which traversed much of the local countryside. We also, of course, solved the crossword.

On arrival in Reading, we would kill any spare time before we felt that we should join the queue at the Palace Theatre. This was located in Cheapside. The queue formed in a sheltered alleyway down the side of the theatre, and we would wait patiently for quite some time for the opening. It always seemed to be quite orderly.

Having gained access and purchased the tickets, we would dash up the stairs to get the best possible position in 'the gods', which was the balcony above the Dress Circle. We saw so many famous music hall acts during those years—Max Miller, Izzy Bonn, Leslie 'Hutch' Hutchinson, Charlie Kunz and Nosmo King. It was claimed that Nosmo took his stage name from the wording etched on a railway carriage window, 'No Smoking'. There were many, many other famous acts. In common with many such establishments, the Palace Theatre closed, and was demolished in 1960.

Not all the activities were indoors of course. As I said earlier, to subsidise the food supplies during the days of rationing, Peter and I did a little rabbitting with ferrets. We had some odd moments with this activity. On one occasion we were at the edge of woodland at the original Coppid Beech Hill. The area was meadowland and woods, which the dual-carriageway and the junction of the A329M, now cover.

Anyway, on this occasion, we were setting down the nets, when we spotted a local policeman leaning on the fence watching us. "Let us appear as if we have every right to be here", was our decision and, after a few minutes, he mounted his bicycle and rode away.

Another time, we were cycling along the Reading Road, with me in the lead, when I heard a cry of dismay. Looking round, I realised that the bag containing Pete's ferret had slipped off his handlebars and spun round in his front wheel. We tentatively opened the bag, expecting a wounded animal, but the ferret poked his head out, looked around and was obviously none the worse for the 'spin'.

In a small copse in Holt Lane, on the same side as the school, we found some burrows and decided to try our luck. Having put a ferret down a hole, we sat for ages waiting for a result. Along came a well known local character, 'Darkie Prout'. Here was a chap that knew all about ferrets etc. He just looked at the hole and said "E'll never cum out. That there is a badger's 'ole. 'E will 'ave killed 'un". Of course, knowing that Darkie was an expert, we rather disconsolately left the scene. Ever since, we have always been convinced that Darkie won himself a ferret that day.

My particular ferret caused an entirely different problem. I was in the Ritz enjoying the film, when there was a tap on my shoulder and Mr. Blake said, "You had best go home. Your mother has a problem". So, of course, I hurried home to Rose Street to be met by Mum and told that the ferret had escaped from his hutch. She had put a bucket over him in the yard.

I was a bit upset, because he would have been quite alright there until I came home after the show. It did demonstrate again how we

64

youngsters were known by the older folk, because Mr. Blake came straight to me in the darkened cinema.

Earlier, I spoke about the racing at Ascot. In our youth, we would on occasions, ride to Ascot on our bikes and leave them in a nearby garden—sometimes for a small fee. Then we would go on to Ascot Heath, where entrance was free. Of course, there were bookmakers to take your wagers, or should that be wages?

'Prince Monolulu', the famous, magnificently dressed tipster, would always be in attendance calling, "Ah gotta horse!", as he sold a supposed winner for the next race. It is my belief he tipped every runner thereby ensuring he tipped a winner. On one occasion Edna came along with us lads and placed a shilling each way on a horse in the last race. It won! Away she raced to collect the few shillings that she had won only to find that the bookie had departed. This was not an unusual practice with these dubious characters, who probably could not gain entrance to the enclosures.

Soon after that event, the bookmakers on the Heath had to work within a fenced area and were not allowed to leave until after the last race had been paid out. I don't think it was Edna's few shillings that forced the authorities' hands!

One very hot and magnificent summer day, Peter, my long time friend, and I cycled to the races and were well prepared with bottles of drink. We were very pleased, as the 'wide' boys on the course were selling made up lemonade for an exorbitant price and it was selling like the proverbial 'hot cakes'.

Mid-afternoon, they had run out of the powder to make up more lemonade. So, not to be beaten, one particular chap near where we sat was filling glasses with water. Because he could not charge for water, he was hiring the glasses at sixpence a time. By this time, our supply of drink was exhausted. So when he went to fill his bucket, we followed him to a tap under the stands and refilled our bottles. We were not to be outdone either.

It seems odd that since those early days, we have not been to Ascot Races. As we know, people travel from all over the country to this racing festival.

There are two other memories of the cycling days. When we were in the Wokingham Youth Club, the membership was rather mixed. There were the ordinary lads of the town, of which Peter and I were representative, and there was another element of 'toffs', for want of a better term.

Anyway, a cycle trip to Windsor was arranged, to meet with another Youth Club there and partake of tea. We set off in high spirits. When we reached Coppid Beech Hill—again, I am speaking of the old road, parts of which are still visible. One of the girls, who came from Winnersh, had a rather elderly 'sit-up and beg' machine. Unfortunately her cycle chain broke.

Everyone was aware of this, but only Peter and I stopped to assist her. We managed to get a piece of wire from a fence and did a temporary repair, which, it transpired, did allow her to ride home.

We carried on well behind the rest of the group, which mainly consisted of the 'upper-crust' and eventually arrived at the venue in Windsor, where we had an opportunity to express our thoughts about their ungentlemanly attitude.

During the war, I would guess about 1943, when we were sixteen years of age, Peter and I decided to join the YHA (Youth Hostel Association). It beggars belief, on reflection, that we decided to cycle to London; in fact, to the hostel at Highgate. We set off in great spirits and I would think that it must have been around the Staines area that we asked a group of workmen if we were on the right road to London. "Just keep going", or some such phrase was used. So we kept going, on what to us was a great adventure.

We did find London, but Highgate was something else. We seemed to go from policeman to policeman to get directions. One such enquiry earned Peter a severe reprimand. We spotted a constable directing the traffic at one of the busy junctions where a number of roads met. He was not impressed with the manner in which Pete manoeuvred between the cars, nor with the fact that he was expected to cease directing traffic whilst he explained the way. We finally made it and booked into the hostel. It was possible to get a late pass key to allow extra time for exploration, but it was very forcibly put to us that the golden rule was to be very quiet when we returned.

We went into the centre of London and decided to partake of the fine food at Lyons Corner House. We ordered sardines on toast and followed by pancakes. The waitress asked us how many pancakes we required and, knowing that the pancakes at home were very filling, we said, "Only one each please". We neither of us realised how thin it was possible to make pancakes.

However, we found our way back to the hostel at a rather late hour and crept up a very dark staircase—here a blunder. Peter mistakenly thought he had another stair to climb, but not so, and he crashed through one of the dormitory doors. We thought it was hilarious, but we were alone in this. When it was time to return home, we rode across London to Waterloo Station and decided, without too much argument, to put our bikes on the train and return home in comfort.

oOo

A Few Years On.

I have always been interested in sport of all types and one of my greatest pleasures was playing football. I had played in the school team, then in the Wokingham Junior Sports Club team.

I was 'called up' in 1945 and joined the Royal Berkshire Regiment, where I served for the next three years. I quickly became involved in any available sporting activity. I played football and hockey for the battalion, plus cross country and track running, and boxing. In fact, anything that would get me released from the awful guard duties, and sport certainly did that.

The one really useful thing that came out of my army service was that I was taught to drive while in Colchester, Essex. During our infantry training period, six of the unit were selected to take a six week driving course. We were taken out each day in 15cwt. trucks and eventually an officer took each of us individually for the test in Colchester centre. Oddly, and in typical army fashion, we were tested driving a 3-ton truck, twice the size of the vehicle we were taught on. Amazingly, all six of us passed the test. This was the first time that had ever happened, we were informed.

Moving from Colchester to Dover Castle, prior to being posted to Germany, I was put into the three inch mortar platoon. Again, in army fashion, given the task of driving a bren gun carrier, which was a small tank-like vehicle with tracks—entirely different to driving a wheeled vehicle. They knew how to confuse us!!

After three years in the army, the great day of demobilisation came along and we travelled across Germany to board a ship at Cuxhaven. We then sailed to Hull and the demob centre to be fitted out with all our civilian clothing. Myself, and a close pal, were quietly taken from the main mob by a typical tailor-like individual to be fitted out with the rather, better than ordinary, chalk pin-stripe suit. Not many of these were issued. He must have chosen us as an easy touch. For, having explained what a great favour he had bestowed upon us, he then held his hand out, which we gratefully shook and walked away.

When I returned to work in 1948, after army service, the print works had been much enlarged and more machinery added. Also, of course, men had been released from the services, so the staff was also increased. It was a different way of life altogether, but I soon settled down again.

There is one little item, which, to this day, still gives me pleasure. When the **W**okingham & **D**istrict Association for the **E**lderly was formed in 1968, Mrs Jean Davey came to Mr. Lee and asked if we could provide letterheads with a logo. I was given the task to find the answer. I took a small gummed label, with rounded corners, and printed out the letters **WADE.** I then positioned them as they appear today, with the A and E dropped below the level of the W and D. The image was then reversed, to print blue with white lettering. I always get a kick out of that small thing whenever I see the logo today, despite having arranged the layout for a great many images over the years.

Whilst I was serving in the army, Edna was doing her duty as a nurse at the Old Windsor Hospital. This, of course, was a different way of life to her previous occupation in the wire rope works. Edna returned to Wokingham some months after me. So bicycle rides to Windsor and back continued to be a feature of my life, as they had when I had been on leave from the army.

Having been demobbed at the age of twenty-one, I then joined the Wokingham Junior Old Boys and played the familiar indoor games and, of course, football. The club was very successful for some time, then members started to look for higher things and many joined the Wokingham Town F.C. I also did that and quite enjoyed playing on the now defunct Finchampstead Road ground.

This ground had been part of my life for many years, because while I was still in my pram, my mother and aunt were regular spectators at Wokingham. I had an uncle, Cecil Case, and a cousin, Hubert Case, playing regularly for the town team. All the players were Wokingham men who played with great fervour, with no thought of reward, except to be winners.

In later years, when I played there, I was in disagreement with some of the committee members. I took my boots over to St.

69

Sebastian's Football Club, where I spent very many happy years, both as a player and on the Committee as Treasurer. I then became Chairman and, finally, President. Sadly, with the coming of Sunday football, the lower leagues of the Saturday game began to suffer and 'Saints' became an early casualty and closed down.

In our youth, a group of us, about eight, played tennis on a Thursday evening at the beautiful courts in Barkham Road. They were situated on land behind the 'Tanhouse'. The owners, Ernest Fidler and Alfred Pollecut, would sometimes step in and give us some impromtu coaching. As was inevitable, developers thought that it would be ideal to build even more of their houses and offered such a good price that it couldn't be refused. That was the end of the group's tennis evenings. At the time, it was very upsetting, but we survived.

It was in the early period of this activity that Edna and I really started a serious courtship. We had known each other all our lives, but we suddenly realised that there was a certain spark, so we ignited it. We found that we were so compatible and knew that at a date in the future, we would tie the knot and spend a happy life together. In fact, we were seventeen at the time and it was nine years before we were in a sensible situation to commit to marriage.

A home of our own was, of course, a top priority and we did look very seriously at a bungalow being offered for sale in Waterloo Road. It was a snip, but before we could make a move, it was withdrawn from the market.

Good fortune smiled upon us, because Mrs. Harold Lee, who owned the ladies dress shop, Primrose Dale, offered us the vacant flat above the shop. We had no hesitation in accepting this magnanimous offer and set a date for the wedding—a date in Coronation year. We never had a moment's doubt that we were an ideal match.

The wedding took place at All Saints Church and we were really dressed for the event. I purchased a new suit and Edna and Beryl, her bridesmaid, travelled to Conners in Reading for a bridal gown—£6, plus £1 for a veil, and the bridesmaid's dress was £4. Just consider the difference today, when a small fortune is needed to provide dresses and suits.

After a week's honeymoon in Torquay, we returned home to find bowls of flowers on every place that could take a vase—even the toilet cistern and seat. Mr. Lee had ransacked his garden to give us a truly floral homecoming—unforgettable. We obviously are not wanderers, because we are still in the flat, happy as 'sandboys'.

When we moved into the flat, we were also given the use of the garden at the rear. At that time, there was no service road. We had apple trees, a pear tree, various soft fruit bushes and lawns. Along the wall—now the far side of the service road, some wonderful forsythia shrubs—always a picture in the Spring. With the introduction of the service road, the garden area was covered with tarmac, to allow for easy delivery to the shops and printing works—a much needed facility. Just imagine large pallets of paper, machinery etc., being moved from the street—not really the ideal situation. Today, the service road is rather a race track with cars entering at the 'No Entry' end, and others illegally turning left into Luckley Path.

One of our very happy memories is of the time when the whole family would attend the speedway, or as we called it, the 'dirt track' racing at California. Mr. Cartlidge, the owner at that time, ran a quite successful leisure park, a miniature zoo, and a train running around the site. There were boats on the lake and swimming was allowed.

But back to the speedway. This was a most popular event on a Sunday afternoon. The crowds would pack in all around the track—many climbing up nearby trees. It was always a quite thrilling spectacle, to see these chaps on their racing motor-cycles, whizzing round the track. There was the never to be forgotten smell of the high octane fuel—most distinctive.

If one knows where to look, it is still possible to pick out the area of the track. It is now overgrown, and some parts quite marshy. The whole site today is known as California Country Park and is a very pleasant spot to visit. Lots of bird-life, nice walks, children's play area and a restaurant.

Anno Domini 1953, Coronation Year, recalls memories of street parties and such. In Rose Street, we formed a small committee and went round the houses every Monday evening collecting coins of whatever value folk could spare. They were generally very generous and, when the day arrived, we had a great time. All the children attending lived in Rose Street or its off-shoots, Queens Terrace, Rose Court, Rose Gardens and Cross Street. What a gathering we had.

Rose Street Coronation party 1953.

There are adults walking around in the town today that recall the event with many fond memories. Another event in the Market Place has to be mentioned here, because it was the last time an ox-roast took place—cooked on a very large spit for many hours and basted by the local firemen. Once carving began, even this large animal was soon devoured. With all the E.U. rulings, it is very doubtful that an ox-roast will ever be held in the town again.

The Ox-Roast.

The day of our wedding in October coincided with the home-coming party for the lads that had served in the Korean War, some of whom had been prisoners. The problem was that we had booked the British Legion hall for the reception, but the Legion had let all the tables be taken for the street party—PANIC! Fortunately Mr. Lee had some sway with the Masonic Hall people and we were able to transfer their tables to the Legion Hall on the Saturday morning, so all was well.

Our wedding day, October 1953.

Within a year of our marriage, we joined the ever growing band of motorists. We purchased a 1937 Ford car for about a £100—a lot of money at that time. It was a good buy, because it had been owned, and serviced, by an engineer at Blackbushe Airfield. It served us well for many years and we travelled the country far and wide—a most enjoyable period.

We also had the benefit of being able to garage the car at 9 Rose Street. Apart from all the rooms and facilities there, the property also had a large brick and slate roofed building, which had, in earlier times, been the stables. There were even mangers along the back wall. When anything needed repairing on the cars, we were able to do the work, whatever the weather, in a cosy environment. We could also do jobs on cars in those days—take out the engine, clutch or whatever—not so today.

We were not the only ones in the family with a car. Father and my brother-in-law, Peter, were also car owners and we seemed to have spells of visiting various areas. For instance, we paid regular visits to the Berkshire downs for Sunday picnics. We then had a spell of travelling to West Wittering for a day by the sea. Here we would set up our area with the cars forming three sides of a square and a hedge, or fence, the fourth.

We arrived very early and cooked breakfast on the Calor gas rings. Then at mid-day mother, who was a great lover of the outdoor life, invariably had a pressure cooker on board and would set about preparing a full Sunday roast for lunch—not a box of sandwiches for us. We also had family holidays.

To see the family move off on one of our camping holidays must have been a rare sight. Those cars had no luggage boots, so everything had to be carried on a rack at the rear and a roof-rack. Dad was not the greatest packer in the world and we sometimes asked him if he would be able to get under any low bridges. He took it in good part.

At this time all roads in Wokingham were two way. It seems quite incredible that one could drive from Broad Street, passing the Town Hall, and then turn right into Luckley Path (Iceland corner). All the roads in and around the town were two way and remained so until the early 1970s. It would be very difficult, if not impossible, to have two way movement with the volume of traffic in the town today.

With the introduction of the one way traffic and the opening of the M4 Motorway, the townsfolk lost one great benefit—the coaches that travelled to Victoria Coach Station in London. They could be boarded at the front of the Heelas establishment, opposite the Town Hall. In particular, many ladies would travel to the Ideal Home Exhibition each year. It was an easy, almost door to door journey.

One important event that should not be left out of this account is the visit of Her Majesty the Queen and Prince Philip on 25th June, 1962. A dias was set up at the Peach Street end of the Town Hall and the crowds were massed along the route. Her Majesty was greeted by The Lord Lieutenant of Berkshire and the Mayor, Dr. Phyllis P. Pigott, who introduced the High Steward, the Marquis of Ormonde, and Lady Ormonde, The Mayor's Chaplain, Revd. F. A. Steer, the Town Clerk, then the Aldermen and Councillors in order of seniority. Her Majesty and Prince Philip then signed the visitors' book. After some conversation with the dignitaries, they entered their car and headed off along Broad Street, bringing to a close a memorable day for the town.

One of the very noticeable things about this visit, was the number of police on duty. They were everywhere. In fact if a parade or some such is taking place in the town today, there are always policemen on duty. Unfortunately, there is a very noticeable lack of men on the beat in the town at any other time.

Not so many years ago, it was not unusual to see constables about. In fact, it was quite a common event to see Sgt. Maurice Hedges and Sgt. Ken Grace patrolling the streets. Indeed, I well remember the days when Superintendent Whitmarsh would walk around the town, probably to check that the force were doing their job in the right manner. The patrolling officer on the night beat would try the doors to make sure they were locked.

On one occasion, Edna and I were sitting cosily in our sitting room, when a light tap on the door was followed by the appearance of P.C. George Wakelin. "Your front door is unlocked", he said. "You should be more careful". At that time we had a door in the alcove of Primrose Dale, next to the shop door. The frontage is completely different today. Anyway, we felt properly reprimanded and apologised to George.

He then continued with—"I've got some tickets, and a coach for the Broadmoor Concert, followed by refreshments in the staff canteen. Would you like to come?". This was one of the concerts by the 'Broadhumourists', the group of patients who put on some wonderful shows. We accepted this offer very readily and George left us with the remark, "I'll drop the catch as I go out".

There is another group of people that are not active in the town these days—newsvendors! At one time there were chaps that stood at their chosen spots in the evening and on Sundays selling the Evening Standard, the Evening News and, of course, the range of Sunday papers.

On my way home from work, I would always purchase the Evening News from Mr. Harry Milam standing on the island by the Town Hall. In earlier days, father had purchasing the Sunday papers really organised. There would be a tap on the front door whereupon he would open the bedroom window, lower the correct amount of money in a wrapper to Mr. Webb, who would then tie the papers and the two comics (which we children had to keep us quiet) to the end of the line. Dad would then draw it up, give us the comics, and return to bed where he and Mother could have a quiet lie in and read. I always thought that to be a very smart move.

During our married life, we have been involved in a variety of activities: members of the Wokingham Colorphoto Society for very many years; Reading Wine Circle; Winnersh Dancing Club, where we learned to dance both Ballroom and Latin—a very enjoyable activity. Now we are much involved in the Wokingham History Group. All in all, we have had some extremely interesting and enjoyable years.

In 1997, I felt particularly honoured to be made an Honorary Townsperson. This equates to Freeman in the days of the Borough Council. The Town Council organised a wonderful evening with the full council and many guests in attendance. This does not happen very often and, over the years, only a very few people have received this distinction. In all honesty I am still trying to fathom it out. Why me? Nonetheless, I am still very proud of it.

We have now passed the fifty year anniversary of that wedding day and it was rather wonderful that, amongst the small gathering of friends to celebrate, was Edna's bridesmaid, Beryl (Slark) Swan and my best man, Wally Miles. It was just a small gathering, because Edna arrived home from hospital at mid-day on the anniversary, following a major operation. We count our blessings that, on the whole, we have had very few problems—certainly nothing insurmountable.

We have enjoyed many lovely holidays, virtually covering the whole of England, Scotland and Wales, plus a trip to Ireland, and a few holidays in Europe. Some of these have been coach holidays and some by hiring a cottage, but the bulk of our trips have been tent camping. This has given us the freedom to come and go as we wish to, wherever we wish. We really have some lovely memories and have a marvellous body of friends. Even now, at this advanced stage, we look forward to more adventures in some shape or form.

We have not been blessed with a family of our own, but we certainly have not been without the love and friendship of children. Apart from relations, nieces and nephews, we also have very close ties with Peter's family. He and his wife Doris have raised seven fine young people and we have always been pleased and proud to have been closely involved with them. Many of this younger generation have raised families of their own and, indeed, many of their children, have become parents now. How things move on!

I think that is more than enough about my/our life memories. What is more important is the change in our town of Wokingham and the people of the town that I knew—lovely characters all.

oOo

Wokingham Past and Present.

The title is one that many residents will recognise. It is the headline that Edna and I have used for some years to introduce our slide shows. Our shows have been presented on many occasions in the town and in many other locations in this part of the county. Perhaps I should first explain the way that this came about.

My brother Graham was interested in photography, and had equipment adapted for him to use a camera from his wheelchair. Being like myself, a member of what at that time was the Wokingham Colorphoto Society, we both became interested in audio-visual work. This is matching a series of slides to commentary. Graham made a series called, 'The Changing Face of a Town', which dealt with the development of the new schools and housing estates etc. I, of course, inherited these slides when Graham died.

Graham the photographer.

Some years later, Edna and I were in the Town Hall viewing a series of pictures of the town. We pointed out to some of the group members there that many of these pictures were misplaced in the named locations. The outcome was that we were invited to join the Wokingham Society History Group. Thinking this could be an interesting thing to do, we joined a rather small body of people who were very interested in, and dedicated to, their various projects. After a few months, it was decided to move into a small room of the Town Hall, to allow the group to expand. It was then that Edna suggested that we should make use of Graham's slides to put together a slide show about the town.

Fortune favours the brave they say. In this case, it proved to be so. There were a good many pictures available of the town over the years. Some went back to the mid-1850s and a fine collection could be gathered from a variety of sources. The most fortunate piece of good luck came about through my boss Harold Lee. We had begun using the lithographic process in the printing works as well as letterpress. Because of his dealings with a Reading firm for all the litho supplies, film, developers, plates etc., he was able to purchase, through the trade, a Kodak single lens reflex camera which was new on the market.

He and I travelled to Kodak's premises to collect this treasure and he soon put it to good use around the town. It was most unusual to take street scenes, but Mr. Lee knew so many people that, if he spotted a friend or acquaintance across the road, he would take their photograph, the subject being completely unaware of this. In so doing he also took a picture of the buildings in the street. This has proved to be most fortuitous, because I have been able to make a slide copy of these pictures, and many others, which comprise the series which we have shown many times to audiences.

Of course, with the pictures, some commentary is absolutely necessary. This entailed many hours of reading, memorising and a certain amount of research which, when added to my personal knowledge of people and places, has come together to form our 'Wokingham Past and Present' slide show. Having compiled the whole, I realised that, in fact, I had used only three of Graham's slides.

The process is ongoing, because although the 'past' pictures do not change, the 'present' scenes change almost weekly.

Following the success of the slide shows, it was suggested that a video of the show would be a nice idea. In 1995 I approached Bob Whitmarsh of Accent Video hoping that this could be achieved. Bob was most enthusiastic and, for many months of that year, we were out on the streets in the early part of the day capturing scenes to match the slides of the old buildings.

This was followed by many hours in the studio editing and compiling the final tape. It is pleasing to note that even after all this time, the video is still selling, and still being sent to people overseas. I shall be eternally grateful to Bob for his patience, enthusiasm and expertise.

As a result of our interest in the history of the town, Edna and I have had visits from people from all parts of the world—New Zealand, South Africa, Australia, America, and other areas including, of course, the British Isles. Most of them are descendants of Wokingham families who are trying to learn about their origins. In the main, we have been able to help in their research, and they have left for home quite happy. They still communicate with us.

oOo

Wokingham Shops in the 1940s.

If you, dear reader, have managed to survive to this point, it is my intention to write a little about the way the town has changed. I say a little, because if we went through all the changes that have taken place throughout the history of the town, we would have the 'Encyclopedia Wokingham'. Choosing a period to concentrate on is no easy task. However, I thought that from my own point of view, it would be nice to write about the time when I left school and went out into the world of working for a living—hence 1940s.

This period will demonstrate how shopping facilities in the town differ so much to those of today. At times I will, no doubt, drift away from the specified period when I write about people that I knew, or know, because these folk normally became known to me when I became involved in the life of the town as the years passed. They were in business at the time of 1940s. It was still the time of the war, of course, but I do not wish to include war stories unless, perhaps, just the odd relevant snippet.

Having given this some thought, I considered the best way to illustrate the changes, would be to move around the streets and name the businesses. Then to give younger people and those residents that have moved into the town in later years a little guidance, I will name the business in each location as it was in the 1940s, and the business as in 2004, which I will put following in brackets, thus (A. N. Other).

The Market Place

Let us start the stroll by moving around the Market Place. North West side— No.1, **The Berks Pharmacy**, chemist (HSBC bank); No.2, **Timothy White & Taylor**, hardware (HSBC bank); No.3, **Talbot's Coal Office** (SupaSnaps); No.4, **A. C. Hambleton**, baker (Imperial Cancer Research U.K.); No.5, **E. A. Bullock**, ironmonger (New Look); No.6, **W. H. Smith & Son Ltd.**, at the rear and upper floor, **Gotelee Printing Works**, owned by Len

Lush, (Halifax Bank); No.7, **H. G. Hawkins**, confectioner and tobacconist, also a local volunteer fireman (Sultan Balti Restaurant); No.8, **The Roebuck PH** (Square P.H.); Nos.9 & 10, **Foster Bros.**, gents outfitters (Burton & Dorothy Perkins); No.11, **Drake & Mount**, corn and coal merchants (Specsavers); No.12, **W. H. Cox**, fruiterer/greengrocer (Johnson Dry Cleaners); No.13, **Johnson Cleaners** (still Johnson), first floor **Edwina**, Ladies Hairdresser (not known); Nos.14-15, **Wheatsheaf PH** (Oddbins); No.16, **Sale & Sons**, florist (Going Places); No.17, **Baker,** hardware (Pictures & Frames); No.18, **International Stores**, grocer (Cargo).

Here begins Denmark Street, so we move across the Market Place. South side—No.19, **Drs. Curl, Smith, Chapman, Rose, Kempton & Smiles**, physicians and surgeons (Peacock); No.20, **Henley Frank Curl,** physician and surgeon, private address (Robert Dyas); No.21, **The Wokingham Club** also Howard Palmer Bowling Club (Edinburgh Woollen Mills/ Market House); No.22, **Ferguson Ltd.**, wines and spirits (Gemma ladies fashions & Ladbrokes betting shop); No.23, **C.W. Rawlings**, grocer (Romans estate agents); No.24, **Geoffrey Bell**, optician (Wellington & Son); No.25, **Red Lion PH** (still Red Lion).

Passage to Cockpit Path; No.26, **Sale & Son Ltd.**, seedsmen and nurserymen (part Abbey Bank/part W. H. Smith); No.27, **Joseph Frisby**, footwear (W. H. Smith); No.28, **E.J. Morcom**, watchmaker and jeweller (W. H. Smith); No.29, **Walker's Stores**, grocer (The New Rose); No.30, **Old Rose Inn,** (The New Rose); No.31, **Barclays Bank Ltd.**, (still Barclays Bank); No.32, **E. Moore**, confectioner (Iceland); No.33, **Colebrook & Co. Ltd.**, butchers and fishmongers (Iceland).

Here is Luckley Path. Cross over to the north east side—No.33a, **Reading & Caversham Laundry**, receiving office (vacant); No.34a, **F. J. Searle**, grocer (Julian Grave); Nos.34 & 35, **Hussey & Son**, ironmongers, and **Boots Chemist** (now vacant). The area of these premises is due for re-development. Few people realise that this is in Market Place.

Here is the passage to Rose Street car park. Nos.36 & 36a, **Reading Co-operative Society** grocer and butcher (Stead & Simpson and Superdrug); No.37, **Bush Hotel** (Principles ladies fashions and entrance to Bush Walk, a modern development built where the outhouses of the hotel were in the 1940s); Nos. 38 & 38a, **Heelas, Sons & Co.**, draper and general house furnisher (Mann estate agent and part of Boots Chemist); No.39, **John Eighteen** fishmonger (Boots Chemist); No.40, **Green Bough** café (John Wood).

That concludes the stroll around the Market Place except for the Town Hall. This period was at the time of the Wokingham Borough Council. At the Town Hall, the Town Clerk was J. H. Elliston Clifton, solicitor and commissioner for oaths; R. R. Hole, F.S.I., surveyor and sanitary inspector; C. A. Nibbs, collector of tolls and Town Hall keeper. Wokingham Fire Brigade: W. B. Martin, Capt. and E. Hawkins, Lieut.

The Town Hall in 1940.

The Fire Brigade operated from the Town Hall and a 'call out' was always an exciting time. These men were all volunteers, many of whom operated businesses in the town centre. An alarm would sound in their homes or business premises, and they would down tools and race to the Fire Station. As soon as the first driver had arrived, an appliance would race away. At that time, of course, the warning of their approach was a loud bell. One of the men would take huge delight, sitting at the front, clanging away on this lovely piece of equipment, enjoying himself to the full. They would be swiftly followed by another appliance as soon as a few more men arrived.

The fire engines stationed at the Town Hall were specially built because the standard chassis of these vehicles built by the Dennis Co., were too wide to go through the doors of the Fire Station (shops are now where the Fire Brigade was stationed). The Fire Station in Denton Road was opened in 1969. The Town Hall is now a Grade II* listed building.

Notes on the Market Place: It is interesting to note that, apart from inns, William Cruttwell and William Gotelee were probably the two longest established businesses in Wokingham. They traded in the Market Place. William Cruttwell is believed to have established his printing works and bookshop in 1775. About 1840, this became the premises of William Gotelee. That building today bears the name Gotelee House, and Gotelee Printing is still trading in Norton Road. The Heelas Company was established in 1785 and closed in 1965. At the closure there was still a Heelas on the board of directors.

The Wokingham Club was a favourite venue with many men in the town. The property was purchased in 1910 by Howard Palmer for the use of the club and as the base for the Howard Palmer Bowling Club.

One of the prominent members in the club's early days was Fred Wells, secretary of the cycling club. He was a brother of H. G. Wells, the world famous author, who would on occasions visit Fred in Wokingham.

There is an interesting feature about the building that replaced that of the Wokingham Club. To the left of Edinburgh Woollen Mills is a fine entrance to the office suite above. That entrance is the original one that belonged to the Club building, and it is all that remains of the building

In 1905, another prominent visitor came to Wokingham and lunched at the Rose Hotel, now The New Rose. He was Signor Marconi, the radio pioneer that sent the first radio waves across the Atlantic—a simple 'S' in morse code (…). He commended the hotelier, Mrs. Churchman, on, "a very fine menu indeed".

Whilst on the subject of The Rose—after I had left school, Mrs Peters, my former teacher, and her husband called at my home in Rose Street but I was out. She asked my mother to tell me that they were staying overnight at the Rose, and would I join them for a chat.

I had never been in The Rose before, but I went along rather nervously and was shown into the lounge at the rear of the hotel. There was a log fire and the settees and armchairs looked very luxurious. We were served refreshments by a waitress, and a very pleasant evening ensued. It was an experience I shall always remember.

During the 20th century, The Rose suffered three devastating fires, but like a phoenix, it rose from the ashes and has continued to serve the public of Wokingham in various guises.

Messrs. Sales, the nurserymen in the Market Place, were very well respected for the quality of their shrubs, trees etc. The company was established in 1818, and it occupied premises that had at one time been the Kings Head public house—a Tudor building. Sadly, it was demolished in the 1970s and the present building erected on the site. If you look at one of the beams at the front, you will see what Mr. Churchman, the landlord, was licensed to sell.

The Green Bough café was a favourite haunt with many of the town's teenagers, many of whom would spend hours over a cup of tea and a bun. Hussey, the ironmonger, was popular with the men folk. It was possible to go into that shop and purchase any small single item. Moreover, the staff would ensure that you were a satisfied customer. (The staff at Wokingham Décor have this attitude.)

Next door was the family grocer shop of F. J. Searle. The coffee was roasted and ground on the premises, and the hams and bacon were superb, as indeed were all the products, which were especially chosen by this family grocer.

Boot's, Hussey, Searle's. Market Place prior to redevelopment.

There were other grocery shops in the Market Place: The Co-operative Society, Clement W. Rawlings (remember my trade bike incident?), International Stores and Walker's Stores. All were held in high regard, and were supported by the people of the town.

In the early 1930s, the manager of Walker's, Ernest Morley, and his wife were robbed at gunpoint for the takings. The culprit was never found. It was a very nasty affair.

Walker's grocery store in the Market Place, all redeveloped.

Also respected, and well patronised, was the baker shop of Hambleton, the fish shops of John Eighteen and Colebrook, and the butcher shops of Colebrook and Co-op.

Mr. Cox always displayed his fruit and vegetables in boxes on the pavement fronting his shop. This often proved to be something of a temptation to the gangs of kids who would dash past the shop and grab apples and oranges, leaving a very irate Mr. Cox fuming and shaking his fist.

Another favourite small shop was W. Baker & Son, which had originally been a picture framing shop. Cecil and Doris baker ran a hardware shop, although Cecil was a painter and decorator, and a volunteer fireman. Many years later, it returned to being a picture framing business, This area of the town had such a variety of businesses. Just consider the choice of grocers, fishmongers and butchers in the Market Place alone.

I am sure that many of the older generation will know the names mentioned, and in some cases, probably knew many of the people personally. I can relate to all of them in one way or another, but let us look at other areas of the town:

Broad Street.

Continuing our route let us move along Broad Street. North east side: No.1, **Stewart & Wimbledon**, cycles and radios (Clark's shoes, new development); No.3, **Dexter & Sons**, baker (Westminster Bank new extension); No.5, **Westminster Bank** (still Westminster Bank); No.7, **J. Watts & Son**, auctioneers (Martin & Pole); No.9, **William Allen**, veterinary surgeon (Bennet's Insurance); No.9a, **Barnes & Avis**, radios, etc; No.11, **F. J. A. Wright**, shipping agent, tobacconist and stationer (Flower Corner); No.13, **Wokingham Laundry Co.**, Receiving Office; No.13a, **R. Toomer** Coal Merchant (The whole is now Learn Direct computer classes); No.15, **S. A. Pither**, butcher (Newbury Building Society); No.15a, **Mrs. Berry**, Ladies Outfitters (Connell's estate agents); No.17, **Rbt. Nelson & Co.Ltd.**, house furnishers, baby carriages etc. (Threshers); No.19, **Chas. K. Foy**, electrician and wireless dealer (Pizza Express); **Miss D. Wescott**,

The Gate House (Wallis House, offices); **Miss Burrell-Smith** Private house (Broad Street Tavern P.H.); **Montague House**, Geo. Basil Readman, private house (Bracknell & Wokingham College); **Miss M. Body**, café (Moss Chemist); The remaining properties to the corner of Rectory Road were all private houses. There are still some private residents, but much is used for offices; **Tudor House** doctors' practice.

Shute End to The Terrace—**Miss Julia Maclean**, milliner (Giggling Spring); **Mrs. R. Warren**, art needlework (private house); **Wokingham Tailor Valet Service**, (private house); **Corpus Christi Roman Catholic Church**, (Guildgate House solicitors offices).

On the opposite side are houses which are still homes plus some office use; No.2, **Mrs. M. Smith**, confectioner (Westend hairdressers).

Returning into Broad Street—**Perkins Bros.**, Garage, Motor Engineers (Rectory Court, offices); Nos.30–36, **Four small cottages**, all private homes. Three are still homes, but No.32 is an estate agent; No.28, **Martin & Pole** estate agent (now a number of small businesses); **The Elms, Thomas Ellison and his four sisters**, (offices); Nos.22-24, **Private Homes** (solicitors' offices); **Markham House** Lt. Col. Fortescue Wells, D.S.O. (offices); **Linfield House** (Lloyds-T.S.B. Bank—new building); **General Post Office** (built on site of earlier post office. Opened in 1932); No.14, **W. E. (Sinclair) Hall,** bookseller, tobacconist, confectioner (Roger Platt); No.12, **Hyatt May**, draper, ladies outfitters (Bradford & Bingley); No.10, **Savoy Cinema** (Nationwide Bank).

Here is **Broad Street Walk** with some business premises. It was at one time just the exit way from the cinema. No.8, **W. E. Exton**, ladies and gents hairdresser, chiropodist, tobacconist and sports goods (offices); Nos.4-6, **Midland Bank Ltd.** (Your Move and Midas Cards); No.2a, **H. Spencer**, greengrocer and fruiterer; No.2 (part), **W. J. Strange**, watchmaker; No.2 (part)-2a, (Prontaprint). This is followed by the Broad Street frontage of H.S.B.C., which was also part of the former Berks Pharmacy. Both stated to be Market Place.

Some notes on Broad Street: No.1, the premises of W. (Bill) Stewart were built in 1881 for William Barnard Mower, a corn merchant, who was Borough Mayor in 1893. Prior to Bill Stewart moving in just before the 1939-45 War this had been the doctor's surgery. The practice then moved to Tudor House, Broad Street.

On the opposite corner of Rose Street, No.3 Dexter. This was a fine timber framed building which, it is believed, may have been The Bell Inn at one time (see following); No.7, Formerly Watts & Son.

As a lad at Lees print works, I got to know Mr. Harold Watts quite well. He was a fine gentleman. Donovan Watts (no relation at all to Harold), was a portly gentleman and the firm's surveyor/draughtsman—a jolly chap.

Behind these buildings, from the 14th to the 17th century, was the Wokingham Bell Foundry, Smyths Place. Many bells for churches in the south of England were cast here. Sadly, none are in Wokingham. This may be the appropriate time to comment on the mistaken belief that bells were cast at Bell Foundry Lane. The name itself certainly appears to say that this was the home of the bell foundry. The fact is that the area would not sustain a foundry which has specific needs. What is known is that Roger Landen, an early owner of the Wokingham Bell Foundry, had a farm on this very ancient route. Because of his connection it was called Bell Founders Lane. Over the years this has become corrupted to Bell Foundry Lane.

If you look at the wall above Newbury Building Society, the name of 'Pither', can still be seen. This was a butcher of long standing and had been the business of Hollis, another butcher.

The Gate House was the home of Miss Dorothy Wescott, daughter of the first Borough Mayor. It was she who returned to the Council the insignia that is now worn, either by the Mayoress, in the case of a lady, or the Mayor's Escort in the case of a gentleman.

The present day Broad Street Tavern was, for many years, the offices of J. H. Elliston Clifton, Solicitor and Clerk of the Borough. His niece, Isobell, followed him in the solicitors business.

Montague House was built by Henry Montague in the 1690s. He was a schoolmaster, and the building has been used for most of its time as a place of education, with the occasional private resident, such as Mr. Readman, in 1941.

The beams of Tudor House were exposed in 1920 after the Grosvenor School for girls moved into Montague House in 1919. The Perkins Bros., who owned the garage and workshops, purchased Tudor House as offices. They stripped off the stucco covering and creeper cladding, and exposed the beams of this fine Tudor mansion. In 1927 the property was owned by an antiques dealer who purchased a few beams from the burnt out Billingbear Mansion to add to the building. The doctor's practice moved in just prior to 1939.

Tudor House, Broad Street.

Although not strictly Broad Street, I think the Police Station is worth a mention. It was designed by Joseph Morris, the County Architect, and built in 1904, by E.C. Hughes of Wiltshire Road. It was then occupied in May 1905. At this time, 2004, its future is uncertain, but there are high hopes that it may be preserved for community use.

It is also worth noting that the land, where the Police Station was built, was owned by the Sale family. With the proceeds of the sale,

Chapel Garden was built as the family home. A plaque on the front displays initials and dates, and today it is the Rectory Road doctors' surgery.

Again not Broad Street, but nearby in Shute End, stood the Corpus Christi Church that was consecrated in 1912. It was a church for barely 60 years before being demolished.

Mrs. Smith, confectioner, at No.2 Shute End, later married again and became Mrs. Parmentier. She was also a caterer and supplied the buffet tea for our wedding, at a cost of 4/6d. a head which equates to 22p.

Back to Broad Street—Perkins Garage at the top of Broad Street was also the base for the construction of Removal Pantechnicons, which were praised from all corners of the country, as being easy to load and unload, and easy to drive. Alan Perkins was the first man to include a skylight in the pantechnicon roof which was of great assistance when light was poor. Another point of interest with the Perkins garage—they had a great deal of red-oxide paint, and to preserve the corrugated roof of the workshops, it was decided to use the paint for that purpose. They then had a communication from the Air Ministry asking them to continue the practice as it was a great guide to pilots passing over the area. So they continued to paint the roof red. Fortunately pilots do not need that sort of guideline today because the garage is no longer in existence.

The four cottages at Nos. 30-36 were built in 1771. They were typical of the small homes of the time. One resident, Mr. Tony Bowden, was born in his present home. Like Edna and myself, he is a true Wokingham resident, and there are many more still in the town today.

Next along at No.28, was Martin & Pole. Many years before, the names had appeared on No.7.

The Elms was a fine building, built in the middle of the 1700s by Thomas Pitt, a former Governor of a province of India. He came home with a very large diamond and, from the proceeds, he had The Elms built as a dower house to Swallowfield Court. The diamond, which is internationally known as The Pitt Diamond, was sold to the French government, and was mounted in the crown for the coronation of Napoleon.

The Post Office has been on this site since the late 1800s, but after a complete rebuild, was opened in 1932 with much pomp. The unusual aspect of this building, is the fact that it is built entirely with two inch bricks. At the right hand corner stands a milestone. This has been located in Broad Street since 1759 when the Windsor Forest Turnpike Trust had the road improved. From then on the coaches had to pay a toll to use the road. Milestones were placed along the route.

At No.10 was the Savoy Cinema—the first cinema in the town. I have spoken about these premises in the main text.

The next major change is at Nos.2, 2a, 4 and 6, where now stand the shops of an estate agent, Midas Cards, and Prontaprint. That is a brief look at Broad Street.

Denmark Street.

Let us continue by going down Denmark Street from the Market Place, along the right hand side, which is the North-West side. Where **Jay Print** is, was a gateway which gave access to the rear of the properties and to the former Drill Hall. No.1, **Perkins Bros.**, cycle and wireless dealers; No.3, **C. Lee & Sons**, bakers; No.5, **Miss Farrow**, Drill Hall Lodge (these three premises are all occupied by Design for Living); No.7, **John Pearson**; No.9, **Harry Shorter**; No.11, **Jas. Hurdwell**.

All Drill Hall Lodges are used as business premises. At the rear of the lodges stood the Drill Hall, which was demolished to accommodate the Tesco Store. The building became The Plaza health and fitness club, Prezzo Coffee Shop and Argos catalogue shop in 2003.

No.13, **P. & J. Trill,** cycle dealer (Hudson Bay); No.15, **Bendall**, baker; No.17, **Gosling**, fresh fish and butcher (now the arched entrance way to the premises at the rear); No.19, **Bric-a-brac shop**, probably better remembered as a china shop (Sue Ryder Charity Shop); No.21, **Wellington Stores**, wines and spirits (Berkshire Windows); No.23, **Prudence**, ladies hairdressing

92

(Retreat); No.25, **Symonds**, boot maker (Taj Mahal restaurant); No. 27, **Weston B. Martin,** baker (Wise Employment Agency); No.29, Vacant in 1941 (The Children's Bookshop).

Nos.31–39, five residential 15th century cottages: **Mrs. Dance, Chas Wright, Reginald Brown, Sidney Gough, Sidney Eamer** (Bang & Ollufson, television and Don Beni restaurant); No. 41, **H. M. Customs and Excise** (Don Beni restaurant. At the rear was Fleet Works, the printing works of Dennis Irvin. The works were demolished); No.45, **The Crispin P.H.** (still the Crispin); No.47, **Private house**, Jim Morris; No.49, **Private house,** Ashley Pick (Both properties are now offices).

At the rear stood the Wire Rope Works where a new office block has been developed on the site. No.51, **M. Brookman**, grocer (this listed building has been completely restored). Next along was the **Wokingham Infant Welfare Clinic** and **Wokingham Memorial Welfare Clinic** (The Red Cross Centre and Job Centre). At the corner of Wellington Road was **Elms Lodge**, the home of **William Bridgeman.** This was demolished, and is now just open space.

Now we will reverse direction and go from bottom to top on the South-East side from Norton Road: Nos.68 – 58. This is a row of private houses which remain much the same today. On the corner of Langborough Road is the Dukes Head P.H.

At this point we can consider the premises at the end of Langborough Road. Just along from the Dukes Head was **White Seal Laundry** which later became **London Bottle Closures**. Opposite was the business of **E. T. Huckings & Sons**, a long established local family building company.

On the opposite corner to the Dukes Head, stood two cottages, which were demolished and the area left bare for many years. The sites of No.48, **Ernest Willets**; No.46, **Chas. Bosher & Sons**, confectioners; No.44, **Mrs. Johnston**, rooms to let. From the corner up to, and including, No. 44, is the Library and Anvil Court (home of the Wokingham Times); Nos.42-32, cottages: **Miss Langley, Daniel Pugh, Henry Bromley, Mrs. Riddell, Mrs. Abel, Frederick Riddell,** (entrance to car park); No.30, **The Lord Raglan P.H.** (still Lord Raglan—now with a longer frontage taking in the site of No.32); No.28, **Miss Reeves**, (Wokingham Tandoori); No.26, **Wm. Teakle** monumental mason (café).

At this point is The Courtyard, now offices, but was Teakle's monumental mason's yard (see notes on Denmark Street); No.24, **Thomas H. Bell**, wireless engineer (Wokingham Photographic); No.22, **Quick Service Shoe Repairs** (Kaanaanmaa). Here is the path to the car park, also the Police Station. **The Royal Exchange P.H.**

Then there was the pathway fronting the Exchange Cottages. Nos.1-5 which were at right angles to the street. The residents were **Arthur Wilkins, Mrs. Hamblin, Mrs. E. Beaven, Harry Lailey and Mrs. Hawkins**. On Denmark Street frontage (cottages) Nos. 18, 16, 14, 12, 10. The residents were **Leslie Hamilton, Arthur Barnes, William Smith, William Randall, Albert Collins.**

The area, including the Royal Exchange up to No.10, is now Inspirations Hairdressers; John Bell carpets; Rossini Italian restaurant; British Red Cross shop and part of Eton Travel.

No.8, **Bates & Cuming**, stationers, newsagents, knitting wools (Eton Travel and Designs for Living); No.6, **Charles Scragg**, fruiterer and greengrocer (Fullers Flowers); No.4, **Misses Rourke & Hayes**, fancy drapers (Country Dry Cleaners); No.2a, **Harry Drinkwater**, (Country Cobbler); No.2, **Ernest Brant** Photographer (Jad'or). This is the top end of Denmark Street.

Notes on Denmark Street: Starting at No. 1, the shop of Eric Perkins. I have already written about the early television experience and about No. 3 Lees Bakery, so let us move on down the road.

The Drill Hall and lodges were all associated with D Coy. 4th Battalion of the Royal Berkshire Regiment T.A. These were the first men drafted in the 1939 campaign and many escaped at Dunkirk. The hall was used for lots of social events in the town— the Carnival Ball, the Mayor's Ball, bird and horticultural shows, and many other occasions. The local lads and lasses spent many happy Saturday evenings at the dances.

A short distance along was one of Wokingham's long-standing family concerns—Trills cycle dealers. This was founded by Clarence Trill in the Ship Inn yard in Peach Street. He was followed by Jack and Pip Trill—two stalwarts of the Wokingham Fire Brigade. They took the business to the yard of the Royal Exchange and finally to the shop where Hudson Bay is today. The Trill Brothers were truly Wokingham townsmen. At the Town Hall can be seen a first class Penny-farthing bicycle that was donated by the Trill family.

Where the arched frontage to the Plaza fitness club, Argos and other businesses is today, once stood the baker's shop of Mr. & Mrs. Bendall. Next door was one of the many butchers and fishmongers— the shop of Gosling. Where Retreat hairdressers is today was, for many years, a public house. It had a variety of names, the last being the Wellington Arms. This fronted the Wellington Brewery which covered a large area of land to the rear of the street frontage premises.

Weston Martin, the baker at No.27, was another fire brigade stalwart and, at one time, Captain. Wes had a reputation for his currant buns. It was said that he put the currants in from the other side of the road and most of them missed!!

The small timber framed cottages housed many local families, but in particular, I often visited Mrs. Dance who lived in the first one. She was the mother of Mrs. Lee, my employer's wife. At lunch time or, as we called it, dinner time, I would leave work a few minutes early to take a meal from Mrs. Lee to the dear old lady. The early start was intended to allow me to get home in Rose Street in time to start my dinner hour. It didn't work out like that because Mrs. Dance saw so few people she would engage me in conversation, just for the company. I did get home for dinner eventually.

At the rear of Nos.47-49 stood the wooden building that housed the wire rope works of the Pick family. W. H. Latham Pick brought the wire rope business from London to Bracknell and thence to a workshop in Wokingham. This was at the rear of today's Specsaver's premises. The move to the Denmark Street workshop, formerly a mineral water works, was made in the early 1920s.

Here they produced wire cables of all sizes, from cycle brake and 3 speed cables, to ships hawsers, of great lengths and thicknesses. The power to drive all the shafts and belts, came from a gas engine which, by all accounts, was a brute to start in the morning. It was a very industrious place, particularly during the war years. Today, the site has a fine new office building on it.

The Red Cross Centre has changed dramatically over the years. The original building was a Primitive Methodist Chapel which, in 1922, became the Memorial Clinic, purchased by public subscription. It was here that the school dentist frightened us all half to death.

Much has been rebuilt, but the small Sunday School building built by the Primitive Methodists in 1902, still survives. Each Armistice Day, the Red Cross and the Wokingham History Group, invite the Mayor to lay a wreath at the memorial stone on the front. Comments about the Clinic and school dentist are in the early text.

Going back up the other side, there is little to be said until the former stone masons of W. Teakle. In the yard, which is now the Courtyard, stood a very ancient barn. This was the mason's workshop, but it really was old. When the development began, the Wokingham Society fought tooth and nail to save this building. Of necessity, it had to be pulled down to allow the development.

However, if you care to walk into the Courtyard, you can quite freely view the building at the far end. It is constructed with the timbers from the ancient barn. It is interesting to study the beams and note the parts of large hinges and other metal fittings, still attached to the beams. So at least its soul remains.

The properties in this area had premises at the rear where families lived. As mentioned in the street review, there were many timber framed cottages that were demolished in the name of progress. In all honesty, I suppose that in the town centre, business premises are vital to success.

From there up to the Market Place the properties have changed very little, but of course the occupants have. The entrance to the left of Kaanaanmaa has a wall on the right with beams displayed, There is also a small window on the upper floor. This was, at one time, a part of the Poor Law Workhouse which closed in 1835. The window was, in all probability, a wooden hatch. If one of the elderly inmates died during the night, the staff would ease the corpse out through the hatch to a waiting wagon. This was preferable to carrying the body through the building past the other residents.

Denmark Street was, at one time, named Down Street. The name was changed in honour of Princess Alexandra of Denmark who married the Prince of Wales. They later became King Edward VII and Queen Alexandra.

We now move into the last of the town centre's three main streets.

Peach Street.

Still concentrating on the period of the early 1940's. Moving from the Market Place on the left hand side. Many people do not realise where the Market Place ends and Peach Street begins.

Nos 2, 4 & 6 J. Snell, Gents Outfitters and Ladies Haberdashery (the whole row of shops in this area was demolished to make way for the concrete structure which itself is due to be rebuilt in the future). To illustrate where No.2 Peach Street was, stand at the doorway of Going Places adjacent to the photographic shop and look directly across the road. That is about where the shop of J. Snell began—the start of Peach Street. All to the left is Market Place. No.8, **J. Bristow,** baker, (later Butchers the bakers). It is impossible to state what is in this location today as changes take place quite regularly. Let it suffice that the reader can judge the spot with reasonable accuracy.

No.10, **F. Alder,** hairdresser. At the rear in No.10a lived **George Flint and family.** No. 12 **T. Evans**, wool shop; No.14, **W. T. Adams**, radio and cycle dealer and television expert.

From this point much is as original. No. 16-18, **W. E. Anstee,** butchers, (Fineweave Carpets); No. 20, **A. W. Trimmer,** fruiterer and greengrocer, (Vitality health foods); No. 22, **S. G. Hussey,**

Bon-Ton ladies and gents hairdresser (mobile phone shop); No.24, **Redan PH**, (still The Redan); No.26, **Somerscales**, fried fish and chips (Haka, Chinese take-away); No.28, **R. Arnold**, newsagent and tobacconist; No.30, **S. Gough**, hairdresser; No.32, **The Creamery**, F. Aldridge; No.32a, **Swift Cleaners**; No.34, **London Central Meat Co.**, butcher; No.38, **Galleon Tea Rooms**, Mrs. G. Plumridge; Nos.28–38 (all Marks & Spencer); No.40, **F. King**, dispensing chemist; No.42, **Mitchell Bros**, tobacconist and newsagent; No.44-46, **Misses H. & E. Dredge**, draper. Martins newsagents, tobacconist and confectioner, now stands on Nos.40, 42 and 44; No.46, (Oxfam); No.48-50, **Herring Bros.** china, carpets etc. (Baranda Restaurant); No.52, **H. Bowyer & Son**, corn merchants, (H. Bowyer & Son, Wokingham Pet Shop).

From this point to Cross Street is all new development from the early 1960s. The following are the premises as in 1940: No.54, **Herring** coach hire; No.56, **Geo. Wigmore**, private resident; No.58, **Singer Sewing Machine Co.** and **Wm. Wheeler,** boot and shoe repairs; No.60, **Mrs. M. White**; No.62, **Cecil Choules**; No.64, **Joseph Mowlem**; No.66, **Mrs. L. Hasler**; No.68, **Miss Milam**; No.70, **Jn Peters**; No.72, **Jas. Millard**; No.74, **Frank Carter**; No.76, **Rbt. Simmonds**; No.78, **Geo. Kew**; No.80, **Mrs. Morrissey**; No.82, **Albt. Franklin**; No.84, **Wm. Smith**; No.86, **Frank Benham**; Nos.88-90, **E. C. Peggs**, dairymen.

Here is Cross Street. After the 1939-45 war a row of prefabricated bungalows was erected in Cross Street. **John Westende Almshouses**, Nos.98, 100, 102, are now demolished and the road entrance widened—also part of the Ship car park. No.104, **Cyril Carter,** motor engineer, now the Ship Restaurant and the **Ship Inn.** Here is the junction of Wiltshire Road and London Road.

We now return on the South side of Peach Street: **John Westende Almshouses** (Nos.83-73) and **Queen Victoria Almshouses** (Nos.71-69) have all been replaced by the Westende flats for the elderly and the new Victoria House. The entrance road has replaced, what was at one time, the entrance to the farm at the rear.

No.67, **Alfred Caiger**, cycle and radio dealer (Sorrento Restaurant); No.65, **Wm. Medcalf** (Wokingham Glassworks); No.63, **David Jones** (vacant); No.61, **Frank Benham,** car and coach proprietor, (Acorn House and Modcomp); Nos. 59-53, are today known as the Overhangs. They are beautiful timber framed buildings that have been preserved by a private owner, a local born gentleman. At the rear, some fine office buildings have been built.

The Overhangs are all offices today, but in 1941, they were private homes. No.59, **Reginald Rowlands**; No.57, **Jas. Holley**; No.55a, **Mrs. Ricketts**; No.55, **Arthur Paice**; No.53, **Geo. Roberts**; No.49, **Jn. Stepp**; No.47, **Hy. Hocking**, confectioner (Teak House Restaurant).

Here is Easthampstead Road. No.45, **Fred Collins**, garage (T. G. Art Gallery and Russell Caulton, opticians); No.43, **Berry & Painter**, blacksmiths (offices); 41-35, **Richardson & Starr**, Central garage (Panasonic, Future Homes, Blue Arrow). Here is the entrance to South Place (see notes on Peach Street). No.33, **The Welcome Inn**. At the rear was the meeting room of the **1st Wokingham Boy Scouts** (Barrett dry cleaners, Prospect estate agents and Millett's).

Jarman's, Woolworth's, Bata etc.

Here is the entrance to the service road. No.31, **Geo. Bailey**, delicatessen (Beijing Chinese take away); No.29a, **Fletcher**, greengrocer and fruiterer (Sally); No.29, **Bata** footwear (vacant. A betting office has been proposed); No.27, **Sanders Bros.** grocer (Lunn Poly); No.25, **Woolworth Stores,** (in occupation since 1936); No.23, **Jarman** confectioner and tobacconist, (Intoto Kitchens). Here was an entrance to a former timber yard which later became the back entrance to adjoining properties. Zappa hairdressers now occupies this location.

No.21, **E. J. Ward**, wallpaper, paint, glass etc. (entrance foyer to offices above Zappa); No.19, **Primrose Dale**, ladies' outfitter (Croc's Toys); No.17, **W. H. Lee**, printer and stationer (West Cornwall Pasty Shop); No.15, **T & E Johnson**, cooked meats and fruiterer (Leighton optician); No.13, **Misses K & R Caiger**, footwear (Woolwich Building Society); No.11, formerly **B & A Meat Co.**, but during the war years used by the National Fire Service as a rest room (George Bowcock footwear); No.9, **Geo. Ford & Son**, corn merchants (Bookends); No.7, **W. H. Brakspear**, beers, wines and spirits (Happy Snaps); No.5, **J. H. Dewhurst**, butcher (Going Places); No.3, **Home & Colonial Stores**, grocer (Going Places); No.1, **Modern** hairdressers, (Ladbroke).

Thoughts about Peach Street which has been altered more than any other. Many of the small shops and cottages were demolished in the early 1960s to make way for the concrete structures that we have today. It must be said that you either love or loath them. If you take the logical view that the cottages did not add to the business activity of the town centre, one must accept that the building of shops would improve the situation. That said, my own opinion is that the design and construction could have been planned to suit an ancient market town using traditional materials. Of course, the cheaper to build, the larger the profit.

In a similar way the demolition of the small shops, from Nos. 2 to 14, and the shops from 33a to 35 Market Place, and their replacement by concrete blocks, is not an attractive feature in the town. Whether the proposed re-development will be an improvement remains to be seen. I have to admit that these thoughts are all my own and others may well disagree.

As in all the areas of the town there were many characters in Peach Street. The two gentlemen who worked in Snells were always so pleased to serve the public. George Lambourn and Ben Freeman would always do their utmost to satisfy their customers, selling the hard wearing clothing in what can only be described as an 'old fashioned' shop. Boxes and drawers would be pulled out to find the items requested and they were not happy until the customers were fully satisfied with their purchase.

The little baker shop of Mr. Bristow (later Butcher the baker) was a lovely place to purchase cakes, bread etc. You were always greeted by a smile and chat.

Peach Street now the site of the Arcade.

Members of the public were well served with hairdressing facilities in Peach Street. There was Modern at No.1; Fred Alder at No.10; Sid Hussey at No.22 and Sid Gough at No.30. Probably the most noted character in the street was Richard (Dickie) Arnold who wrote many comical verses in the Carnival programmes, mostly to help advertisers to sell their wares.. He also wrote other pieces which were well received by the people of Wokingham.

Mr. Herring not only served the public from his shop, he also had coaches (char-a-bancs) garaged at the rear of the cottages nearby. It was quite usual for these coaches to be hired for seaside

101

trips etc, although, of course, during the war this was rather curtailed.

Without doubt, Stanley Bowyer must be included as a character. He was voted on to the Borough Council as a very young man and continued for most of his adult life, serving the inhabitants of Wokingham.

He influenced the life of the town in many ways. I consider that one of the most important contributions he made, was being a leader of the group, that in 1949, led Wokingham out of the age of gas lighting in the streets to the wonderful improved fluorescent lights. What a magical change. It made the streets much safer for walking, driving, etc. He was twice Mayor and also a Freeman of the Borough. At the same time he gave first class service at the pet shop in Peach Street—a remarkable man.

Switching on the fluorescent lights Sept. 1949.

As already stated, the remainder of Peach Street was mostly cottages down to the Ship Inn. The exceptions were Mr. Wheeler, the cobbler, who spent each working day sitting just inside the front window of No.58, repairing boots and shoes. He looked straight down Easthampstead Road which, until the late 1800s, was called Star Lane. Hence, when you cross the railway, you go over Star Lane Crossing.

A little further along Peach Street, at Nos.88 & 90, the Peggs Dairy operated. Today, of course, all the residential premises have disappeared. I wrote about the cattle moving through the town and down Rose Street in the early text. This also happened in Peach Street. The area that is the car park off Easthampstead Road behind the Westende flats etc., was at one time farmland. The cattle would be herded along the dirt track—now a tarmac drive next to the Sorrento Restaurant, and driven up to the dairy owned by the Peggs family until its closure in the late 1940s.

Returning to the 'characters' theme, Cyril Carter who operated in the workshop at the rear of the Ship Inn can only be described as a loveable rogue. During the period of petrol rationing in the last war, if anybody was in desperate need of fuel, a visit to Cyril would usually solve the problem. He seemed to be able to magic coupons from thin air. He was not alone in this because his great pal, Frank Benham, had the same ability. It must have revolved around the fact that they were both involved in the motoring trade. One was an engineer, and the other a hire car and coach proprietor. Their vehicles could be hired for trips to the coast or wherever. Both were well known Wokingham men.

At No.67, was the radio and cycle shop of Alf Caiger. When Eric Perkins decided to retire from his Wokingham Radio Relay business, Alf took the project over. On one occasion when I was in the shop, he invited me through to the rear to see the operation. It was an amazing scene—valves and electronic equipment crammed the room—all buzzing and bleeping away. Having been into Sorrento's restaurant since, and seated in the furthest area to dine, I have tried to visualise the scene. Of course it just cannot be done.

On the corner of Easthampstead Road is a new building in which are the premises of T.G. Art Gallery and opticians. Here once stood the motor-cycle garage of Fred Collins. This was the meeting place for many of the young men in the town, if only to stand and admire the machines.

Next door was the smithy of Harry Berry and Freddie Painter. Even at that time many horses were still being used as working animals as well as for hunting and leisure riding. This was a very busy place and a fascinating attraction to the town's children. They would stand in the open doorways to watch the shoeing operations and the forge roaring away in the rear of the workshop.

Next along was the Central Garage owned by Messrs. Richardson and Starr. They also owned the garage in London Road. The Central was very handy to fill up and there were good repair facilities as well—all gone and redeveloped. At the rear of the garage was South Place, the row of cottages that, until 1831, had been a silk mill. It was, in fact, the last mill in the town to close. Again the whole has been demolished and replaced by characterless brick building.

The Welcome Inn was one of the town's popular pubs. Not only was it well used as a drinking place, at the rear was a good sized room which could, and was, hired by various groups in the town. For quite a long time a group of us had hired the room on Thursday evenings to play table tennis. Nothing serious—just friendly games.

It was on one such evening that we met in a very sorrowful mood. 'Stunned' is the word that comes to mind. February 6th 1958, the day of the Munich air crash, when Manchester United lost so many talented players, and others suffered terrible injuries. We mostly sat and talked. Nobody was in the mood for playing games.

Crossing over the service road off Peach Street came what must have been the first major development in the town centre for very many years. The small shops and town houses in this area were demolished and the block of shops, which includes the Woolworth store, was erected in the mid-1930s. Although many occupants have come and gone over the years, the buildings remain today, just as they were built.

The corner foyer and part of Zappa was where Ted Ward operated. He sold all house decorating materials and, at the rear, were the buildings that, at one time, had been a silk mill. For some years they were the location of Ridat engineering works. What had been Ward's later became The Imp restaurant.

Crocs Toy's has accommodated a variety of occupants. Before the 1914-18 war, it was a saddler and harness maker, later tea rooms and, in 1935, it became Primrose Dale ladies outfitters. When that closed it became Toyworld, very much enjoyed by children and probably dads as well.

West Cornwall Pasty Shop was for some years Millin's, then Jones. After that the front shop was the newsagent, toys etc., of W.Harold Lee, who also ran a very busy print works at the rear, as had Jones and Millin before him. Today, in 2004, the printing works is still in operation, managed by Bryan Lee, son of Harold, it is not as busy as it once was. The capacity for companies to produce work on computers and printers has made a huge impact. Here at No.17 I spent my working life.

Now we come to the little cooked meats, pies, and vegetable shop of Mr. and Mrs. Johnson. Living close by I often chatted to Mrs. Johnson, whose shop was mostly patronised by the wealthier community of the town. Mrs. Johnson always had a cat in the shop, and this furry animal spent much of the day lying in the window amongst the various goodies. Mrs. Johnson once told me that when she trimmed the cooked meats she would put the trimmings in a bowl under the counter. The cat would never go hungry because he could help himself. She put what he didn't eat into rissoles for the next day. The mind really does boggle!

Right to left: Mrs Johnson's cooked meats and Lee Printer's.

The next little shop was the business and home of the two Miss Caigers who had wonderful personalities. They were born in these premises and spent their whole lives supplying boots and shoes to the populace of Wokingham. Mothers would take their children in for fitting and, if either of the Miss Caigers said they were a good fit, the mother was happy with that. They knew how experienced these two ladies were.

The sisters were a complete contrast in appearance although both wore blue and white gingham overalls in the shop. One was short and dumpy while the other was rather tall and stern in appearance. They were kindness itself. They were also very able to deal with their affairs. When the whole block became vacant, except their shop, developers tried to talk them into selling but they would not be swayed. They said it was their livelihood and home and they would retire from it when it suited them and not before.

Misses Caigers' shoe shop.

On occasions they would relate stories to me of their experiences, and there is one which I feel is worth repeating. They needed an outbuilding to store excess stock, so plans were drawn up and submitted to the then Borough Council. The Planning Committee would not pass the plans, so the Miss Caigers invited one of the senior officers of the council to visit their premises to view the situation.

When they showed him the staircase with boxes of shoes stacked up on each side of the steps, he was horrified at the risks these ladies were taking. He went back to the council and explained the situation, whereupon the plans were reviewed and passed. What he did not know was that they had a second stairway and never used the one with the boxes of shoes. They were a canny couple.

The next shop along had a rather chequered history—a grocer, a cycle and motor engineer, a butcher shop and, during the 1939-45 war, it was a rest room for the firemen. After the war Sidney Gough moved from his original shop to this location and it remained a hairdressers until the new development—now George Bowcock's shoe shop.

Bookends was for many years the shop of Geo. Ford which was previously located in Broad Street. Ford's was a corn and seed merchant, but over the years it gradually changed to become almost entirely a garden shop under the management of Roy Benwell.

No.7 was the shop of W. H. Brakspear, the brewer from Henley, which sold wines, spirits and beers. Today, the Happy Snaps photo shop is here. George Flint managed the butchers shop of Dewhurst which was located at No.5.

Next along, at No.3 was the Home & Colonial grocer's shop. It was one of the many grocery stores in the town before the coming of the super-markets. One of the well remembered joys in this shop was to watch the butter being prepared for the customer. A lump was chopped from a large block of fresh butter, and the shop assistant would then shape the piece with butter pats—two small wooden paddles. He would then impress a decorative design with a wooden mould—maybe a thistle, a cow or whatever. It was a fascinating operation to watch.

Finally, at No.1, was Modern the hairdressers, the premises of S. Collins.

I hope this has not become totally confusing but I have tried to give a flavour of the street as it used to be.

Reflecting on this period in the town, and for many years before and after, shopping was totally different. Sunday shopping was unknown. At Easter time, shopping for fish and hot cross buns from one of the many fresh fish shops and bakers on Good Friday morning was accepted. The Ritz cinema never showed a film on that day, and later in the day, an all denomination religious service was held in the cinema.

oOo

Around the Town

I feel that there have been so many changes on the outskirts of the town that a piece covering that aspect is worth including. The shops and businesses that were once so much a part of life have disappeared during the years following 1940. Where to start? The London Road would seem to be a good point. Then we can move around the town in a clockwise (roughly!) direction.

A short distance along the road on the right hand side, opposite the church, was the small general stores of Mr. Claude Kingston at No.27. About one hundred yards (approx. 90m) along, was the confectionery shop of Mrs. Anne Whittingham at No. 45.

We then move down to the corner of Seaford Road where there was the shop of Frank Wm. Purver, universally known as Colonel. He was a small, but jolly little man, who delivered bread around the district in a motor van. Across to the other corner of Seaford Road was the grocery shop and post office of James Bennett. Then Arthur Cardrick, motor engineer, who was next door to the garage of Messrs. Richardson & Starr. The large garage and shop complex covers all of this corner site today.

London Road is rather long, and it would seem reasonable to move along Seaford Road now. Perhaps the School of St. Crispin should be noted before we move off. The school was opened by the Secretary for Education in 1953, and it is the prototype for similar schools around the country. For that reason it has a Grade II listing status.

So into Seaford Road which was completely residential. Many craftsmen lived here, but no businesses. Of course the road curves round to finally join Wescott Road. Soon after the bend we can turn left into Goodchild Road. Here again it is mostly residential with the names of well known, prominent, local families.

However, there were two businesses here. At No. 22, was the shop of Frederick Palmer. It is odd that I remember this as Ted Palmer, a baker. Also there was, at No.24, Herbert Tanner, coal merchant.

School Road runs between Goodchild and Wescott Roads and, of course, one side of the road is all the school property. At the corner of School Road and Wescott Road was the shop of Oscar Hall. It was a busy general store and sweet shop, and so close to the school. Officially this was in Wescott Road, so that has to be the next road to explore.

Just across the road from Hall's was the little general store of the Misses Annie and Emily Beale at No.62. On the corner of Seaford Road was the business of Enoch Street, coal merchant. Moving along towards Easthampstead Road, at No.19, was Gilbert Reed and Elders Dairy. Right to the top of the road, at No.1, was the shop of R. G. Nichols, a general store, but very well known for supplying paraffin oil.

At this point we reach Easthampstead Road. Again, this has always been mainly residential, as is common with the streets around the town. Businesses were very scattered, but in their day, they were vital to the life of the community. On the south west side at No.2, The Victoria Arms public house, which is still flourishing. Strangely, it is now named the Victoria Bar. It is a shame, to my mind, that the long standing public house names are gradually disappearing around the town without any apparent reason.

At No.7, Joseph Jordison, general store, now a Chinese take-away. Next door was the Ritz Cinema opened in 1937. It was at that time the height of luxury and said to be one of the finest in the south. A new building, a bingo hall, stands on the site today. At No.41, was the shop of Edward Rance, confectioner. The last business on that side of the road, if I may refer to it as such, was the Presentation Convent at No.73—a school for young ladies.

On the North-East side is All Saints Church House. The foundation stone was laid in 1901 by Mrs. Howard Palmer of Heathlands. The hall has been much used for various events over the years. At No.54 was a small grocer's shop, occupant unknown in 1940, but later the ambulance station of St. John. This was situated on the corner of Goodchild Road. Today a dental practice.

There are no other business premises in the road, so the next move has to be along Murdoch Road—all residential, and into Langborough Road. Here, at No.36, could be found the shop and Post Office of William Fidler—later taken over by Albert Andrews. Near the bottom of Langborough Road were the workshops of E. T. Huckings & Sons, builders. Opposite, there was the White Seal Laundry and, on the corner, The Dukes Head, proprietor William Rands. He also ran a second hand and bric-a-brac business in the yard at the rear.

Moving into Finchampstead Road, a short distance down the hill on the left, we come to the offices of the Yorktown & District Gas and Electricity Co. Today, this is Beacon Hill Lighting. At the rear the Gas Works were in operation and many of the youngsters in the town would visit the yard of the Gas Works. For a very small sum, a sack of coke could be purchased, which we would trundle back up the hill on our home made trucks to keep the home fires burning.

Then on the corner of Carey Road was the depository of E. W. Reeves, removals. Today, this is the Offices of Berkshire Ambulance call service. Ernie Reeves was a lovely man. A Londoner by birth, he never lost the common touch. He was Mayor of Wokingham and Freeman of the Borough. He and his wife were very respected residents of Wokingham. Ernie had come to Wokingham at the instigation of Isaiah Gadd to manage his removal business. When Gadd died he took over the reins and was a very successful man. The last property on the left, before the railway bridge, was the garden nursery of Samuel Sallery—a busy place.

Going under the bridge and further along on the left, where today stands the garage, was a small group of businesses. They comprised W. T. Adams, wireless dealer, who also had a shop in Peach Street, and Eddystone Garage, the coach hire business of Brimblecombe Bros. Many of the local football clubs hired a coach from here to travel to away games. Very few had their own transport at that time and coach hire was quite reasonable. Next to the garage was the little grocery shop of Ernest Cox.

111

Before the second bridge—the Padson Kennels, Mrs. Yalden-Spencer and Miss Stubberfield. Just before the bridge was the builder's yard of Sidney Charles Berry. This area is now the site of the Tesco store.

Here must be mentioned one of the most important changes to the town—Molly Millars Lane, just beyond the second bridge. In 1941, the only development was at the Barkham Road end, where there were ten houses or bungalows. The rest of the lane was just that—a dirt lane. Model Farm, owned by Mrs. Collingborn, was long established.

Today, the whole area is a vast and very successful business estate, and Molly Millar, whoever she was, is long forgotten. That said, I was recently introduced to a young lady who was visiting the town from the United States. She wanted to see what she could discover about Molly Millar whose name and location she had discovered on the Internet. The family were passing through on their way to Europe and they made a stop in the town. Just by chance I met them. The name of the young lady?—Molly Millar!!

In nearby Eastheath Avenue was a very important industry—the brickworks of Thomas Lawrence. There was a rail track from the site to join the main Crowthorne line on the station side of the former football ground. Many local men worked at the brickyard, and it has been claimed that there is no city in the world that does not contain some Thomas Lawrence bricks. Certainly our own Post Office was built with two-inch bricks from the company.

A little further along Finchampstead Road is Evendons Lane where the Gladys's general store served the local community. Sadly Gladys died a few years ago and her shop was converted into a cottage. Evendon's Store still operates. The butcher's shop of Cecil Belcher also served the local residents for many years.

We now retrace our steps on the left of the road towards town. Between the bridges, first stood the premises of the Mid-Wessex Water Company. Then came the fine old Pin & Bowl public house, followed by a row of nice, comparatively recently built bungalows standing high on a ridge. In No. 43 was Mr. Charles Walker, an undertaker who had a long established business.

On the land behind the bungalows was the Wokingham Town Football Ground with the entrance just before the bridge. In fact that entrance is still there, but all the area between the bridges has been developed with business premises and houses. As mentioned earlier, the football ground is now an housing estate.

Up to the corner and along Wellington Road was once grazing land and fondly called the Carnival Field. This was once part of The Elms estate owned by the Ellison family. Today the area is given over to business premises and the indoor Carnival Pool.

Opposite, in Elms Field—another area of pasture land, is a large, but quite ugly building. It was erected in 1965, by the Borough Council as offices. At the time, it had the distinction of being nominated as one of the best designed buildings, and also, of being one of the worst designed buildings in the country. Today, it is in the hands of the District Council, and in full use. Most of Elms Field has been taken over for various uses.

Moving across the road again and into Churchman's Bit stands a large building with a variety of activities including Ten-pin Bowling, bars and restaurants. Then we come to the very long established, Wokingham Cricket Ground. This is a lovely facility for local cricketers, and long may it continue to be so. It would be a great shame if it should go the way of the football ground. Next along are the well used tennis courts.

The Edward Court Hotel is a comparatively new development but I suspect I would be surprised at the length of time it has been there!

On the corner of Wellington Road and Station Road once stood the busy Metalair factory. During the war years parts for aircraft were manufactured here. After the war other items, such as lawn mowers, kept the works going for some years, but finally it closed and the building became quite derelict. Now the area is fenced off with some small trees in tubs in the space.

Here I have a dilemma—which way to go? I think in order to cover all that I would wish to, it will have to be Barkham Road, then Oxford Road and later come back to Station Yard as it was in the 1940s. So we will travel just a short distance along Barkham Road.

In this road there were just a few small shops and, tucked away in the yard behind No.4, was the market shed of H.E. Hall & Son. It was a very popular venue for folk to gather, both to seek bargains, to socialise, and to be entertained by Garney Hall, as he auctioned off the items. Here was a very colourful Wokingham character—Arthur Garnett Hall. He would stride around the town beaming at all and sundry, waving his walking stick in the air and bellow a friendly greeting. They don't come like that today.

At No.6 were Kirkby's Stores—proprietor Frederick Pocock. This was a grocer and sub-post office which later became Shale's butcher shop. At No.22 was the shop of Joshua Parkin, and the last shop on that side at No. 26—the baker shop of William Crocker.

There was very little on the opposite side—The Three Brewers public house, and on the corner of Oxford Road—the business of Drake & Mount, coal merchants.

We will venture a short distance into Oxford Road. At No.6 was Eli Stevens, hairdresser; at No.16, the shop of David Gilbert. This was next door to one of the many public houses in Wokingham that have closed—The Rising Sun, on the corner of Havelock Road. On the opposite corner were the builders, Messrs. Marfell & Horlick, and then A. C. Barnes Garage.

At this point it is worth mentioning that the first railway lines were laid down for the trains serving the Guildford area in 1849. In 1856 the track was laid to Staines and eventually to Waterloo Station. This of course signalled the decline of the horse drawn coaches through the town and had a devastating effect on some of the coaching inns.

Crossing over the railway we come to the busy Station Yard with the businesses of Minchin Bros., who dealt in corn, poultry food and forage. Next, the coal and coke yard of G. W. Talbot & Sons, and also the taxi business of Thomas Mason, which had a very appropriate telephone number—'Phone Four One'. On the station platform, on the down line for Reading, the newsagents W. H. Smith had a bookstall.

Moving up Station Road, on the left hand side in the early forties were the businesses of The Railway Hotel, built when the railway came to town; The Wokingham Laundry Co. Ltd.—now the location of Alderman Willey Close; William Walden, watchmaker; J. Hopkins, carriage makers; Ministry of Labour Employment Office (with the premises of The British Legion at the rear); F. W. Prater, blacksmith; Hope & Anchor PH; and, at the corner, St. Paul's Parish Room—one of many developments financed by the Walter family of Bearwood.

Just to finalise Station Road—back at the bottom, next to Metalair, was the office of H. E. Hall & Sons, estate agents; next along, J. Gray, confectioner; R. Hosler, heating engineers and ironmongers. A short way up the hill at Beechcroft were the dentists, Wm. Willey and Jn. Inman. A dental practice still operates here.

There is much of interest along the Reading Road. It seems worthwhile to travel as far as Woose Hill Lane (that is how it was named in 1940) on the left and Emmbrook Road on the right.

On the south-west side the tower, named Clock House, is a fine bell tower built in 1893, which fronts the Parish Room already mentioned; then St Paul's School built in 1866—again financed by the Walter family of Bearwood. Some years later, this whole development was bought from the Walter Estate, by Thomas Ellison of The Elms in Broad Street, and presented to the parish of St. Paul. A short way along is St. Paul's Church, consecrated in 1864— another Walter development.

Passing Oxford Road we come to Emmbrook House and the hunting stables of Geo. Vincent Francis. He was the father of the world famous author, and former national hunt jockey, Dick Francis; then William Smith, cattle breeder, and the Reading Road Dairy. At the corner of Woose Hill Lane, was Dougie Thompson, motor engineer—a skilled and popular man.

Cross over to the opposite corner to the Rifle Volunteer public house. To the right of that, was the small shop and sub-post office of Frederick Lee (this shop is still operating in 2004); five small cottages; the offices and printing works of the Wokingham Times; the Brookside Works of Froud & Barrett, builders; Frank Heelas at Mill House; Fras. Cartman at Emmbrook Farm.

The small cottages still survive, but all the other properties in this area have disappeared. The whole has been taken over by a car services and car sales area. Then followed much residential property, until opposite Oxford Road, at No.83, the confectionery shop of Geo. Webb.

Moving on to the area almost opposite the church, stood Beches Manor Hotel—a very fine building of much historic interest, set in seven acres of landscaped gardens. In the late 1950s, it suffered some fire damage, but was by no means destroyed. The owner was instructed to have the building restored because of its historic importance. Instead, the demolition workers were called in to demolish the house. The owner became the first person to be taken to court for such an action, and was fined £100—a derisory amount.

'Beches' a Jacobean manor housed dated 1684.

Now let us return to the town after this tour around. We must just look at Shute End and The Terrace. In Shute End was the former St. Paul's Rectory. This was another Walter development. It was built in 1869 and purchased by the Wokingham District Council in 1938 for use as Council offices. Further development to extend the offices took place in the 1980s. Interestingly, the original Rectory was built entirely with 'header' (end-on) bricks. Take a look as you pass by.

Through the archway at No.12, and at the rear, Charles K. Foy had his business, and was listed as a wireless dealer. He later moved into Broad Street, and finally into Market Place. Haye & Son, solicitors, were at No.8, and at No.2, Mrs. Marjorie Smith, confectioner.

The north-west side is mainly The Terrace. Without doubt, it is one of the finest stretches of preserved properties in the town, and a most attractive feature to visitors approaching from that direction. Along The Terrace proper the buildings are all listed.

No.39, Fernleigh House, was the home of William Thomas Martin, the developer of Martin's Pool, spoken of earlier. The Queens Head public house is believed to be the only building in Wokingham with a cruck frame. At No.15 this building is stated to be the oldest house in the town. Despite its modern frontage it was built in the early 14th century. J. B. Hall & Son, undertakers, were at No.9. This business is still operating under that name in the Finchampstead Road, in the premises that for many years was W. Ham the baker. At No.5—Brown & Sons, builders. Both these businesses had rear entrances off Milton Road.

Moving towards the town we come to what was the Corpus Christi Church which stood for barely sixty years. It has been replaced by development, which to me, seems totally out of place for this area. Guildgate House is a stark red brick building. At 3a, also rebuilt, was Wokingham Tailor & Valet Service, proprietor L. Robinson. At No.3, Mrs. Warren, art needlework. Then at No.1, Miss Julia Maclean, milliner.

At the top of Broad Street turn into Milton Road to view the fine Baptist Church. This has had some modern addition but is a very nice building. Just left of the main entrance is a datum point and this is said to be the highest land point in Wokingham town.

That has taken us all round the town although I expect there will be people that feel something has been missed. I have no doubt that is the case.

Having 'walked' around the town considering the shops etc., the thought comes to me that one of the simple joys in life has become less popular than it once was. Early on I spoke of the walks across the meadows in the 1930s. This activity gave a great deal of pleasure to many families and couples. The flowers, the hedgerows, the birds etc. all combined to make for a pleasant afternoon or evening. Sadly much of the land, as I pointed out earlier, has been lost to housing development—and of course, when most people venture forth—out comes the car.

Do many people now walk across the fields at Pebblestone, or round the local lanes? It is certainly not as easy as it once was. Think of walking from the town and following the road round Emmbrook to the Reading Road. Cross over to stroll along Chestnut Avenue, with very few houses set well back from the lane, and an abundance of chestnut trees all along the avenue.

Autumn time saw many folk gathering the nuts. Sadly there are only a few chestnut trees in the avenue now. Alternatively one could walk along the track of Woose Hill Lane, passing the occasional farm or cottage to reach Barkham Road. If feeling very energetic, turn right, and walk through Limmer Hill.

There were so many tracks and by-ways available to explore. Many are still there but are no longer the quiet places they once were. It is said to be progress. I am not so sure!

All around the town development is taking place—small estates, the rear gardens of houses along the roads, and large developments such as Keephatch. This follows the major developments since the 1950s—Norreys Estate, Beanoak, and Woosehill. All along the Reading Road, in areas of land behind the houses fronting the road, development goes on apace. Some of this is due to take place on flood plains, so there is much concern from long established residents who can visualise severe trouble in the future. Homes are desperately needed by the growing population. There is no easy answer.

The added serious problem that grows with the housing is the volume of traffic. There has been much talk over the years about making the town centre a pedestrian area. That sounds fine, but where does the traffic go? Difficult indeed!!

Wokingham's Listed Buildings and Objects.

There must be a number of people who have an interest in the listing of buildings etc. in the town. There are in excess of 300 items, mostly buildings, and a few other items. For instance, the mile stone at the post office is listed. It was placed as a marker for coach-drivers on the route to London in 1759 when the Windsor Forest Turnpike Trust improved the road and charged a toll for its use.

There is the Wokingham Berkshire / Wokingham Wiltshire marker at the bottom of Rose Street, the red telephone box and the horse trough at the Town Hall. The Beaver Monument in the churchyard, just to the left from the entrance gate. There are only a very small number of similar monuments in the country. The Mollony tomb approximately 14 metres north of the tower.

For listing purposes a building has to be rather special, either in its design, its antiquity or its uniqueness. There is one other reason for listing, and this is known as 'group value'. An application has to be submitted to English Heritage complete with photographs and a written statement of the details. A decision is then made which is not always favourable.

The status rating has been changed in recent years. At one time there were three grades. The lowest was Grade Three, rising to Grade Two, then Grade One. Today the rating is still at three levels Grade Two, Grade Two* and Grade One.

Wokingham has only one Grade One building and that is the former Lucas Hospital at Chapel Green. At present this is being converted into a private dwelling, hopefully being carefully watched over by the responsible bodies.

There are eighteen Grade Two* properties. The most recent addition to these is the Town Hall which was given the grade in 2003. This is a lovely building which replaced the former timber structure, commonly called the Guild Hall. This was demolished in 1858 and the present building was constructed on the site at the cost of £3503.5s.6d. The main part of the cost was met by the County Police, and the remainder by public subscription. It was initially the Police Station and also for the use of the Council.

The main hall was also a courtroom and, as most of the townspeople know, there are cells in the courtyard below. The Town Hall was opened by the High Steward, Richard the 4th Lord Braybrooke, on 6th June, 1860. The present High Steward, Lady Elizabeth Godsal, is a descendant of Richard, and is the first female High Steward of Wokingham.

Other Grade II* buildings.
Broad Street: The Elms, Montague House, Tudor House.
Market Place: No. 6 Gotelee House, No. 25 Red Lion P.H.
Reading Road: No.40 "Littlecourt", (WADE Centre). The church of St. Paul.
Rose Street: Nos. 33, 35, 35a, 37, 39, 80.
Shute End: No. 6, No. 10 (Shute End House).
Warren House Road: Ashridge Farmhouse.
Wiltshire Road: the Parish Church of All Saints.
Finally the outbuildings of Lucas Hospital at Chapel Green. All important buildings deserving the II* rating.
Grade II buildings.
Broad Street: Nos. 7, 9, 11, 13, 19, 27, 29, 35, 37, 39 Oxford House, 41 Colbourne House, 12a-14, 20 Markham House plus railings, Nos. 22, 24, 28, and the four cottages 30-36.
Denmark Street: (East side) Nos. 2, 4, 6, 8, 8a, 10, 22, 24, 26, 28, Nos. 1 & 2 The Courtyard, No. 30 Lord Raglan P.H. (West side) Nos. 31, 33, 35, 37, 39, 37, 39, 43 and 45 Crispin P.H, 47 and 49 for group value, 51 and 53. (South side) Duke`s Head P.H...
Easthampstead Road: Nos. 3, 5, and the southern section of the Victoria Arms P.H.
Finchampstead Road: No. 68 Southbrook.
Glebelands Road: "Glebelands" and associated buildings.
Holt Lane: Holt School.
Keephatch Road: Keephatch Farmhouse, Dowlesgreen Farmhouse, Keepers Cottage.

London Road: St.Crispin's School this fact is often met with dismay but in fact this Wokingham school is the prototype for similar schools throughout the country and has been granted listed status on that basis.

Luckley Road: Luckley-Oakfield School.

Market Place: Nos. 2, 3, 4, 5, 7 & 8 Square P.H. 9, 10, 15, 17, 22, 23, 24, 30 The New Rose, 37 frontage of Bush Walk (formerly Bush Hotel).

Milton Road: Wokingham Baptist Church includes gates and walls. Nos. 2, 4, 6, 8, 12.

Peach Street: *North side*, Nos. 48, 50, 52, 104-108 Ship Inn, *South side,* No. 45, Nos. 53, 55, 55a, 57, 59 The Overhangs.

Rectory Road: The former Police Station. *South East side* Nos. 1 & 3. Part of Colbourne House.

Rose Street: *North West side,* 2 Wingmore Lodge, Nos.4, 6, 8, 10, 12, 14, 16, 18, 32, 34, 36, 38, 40, 42 44, 44, 44a, 46, 48, 50, 52 & 54, 56 & 58 Metropolitan P.H., 68, 70, 78, 82, 86, 94, 96. *South/East side,* Nos. 25, 27, 29, (33-39 II*) Virginia Cottage and Endon Cottage, Nos. 63, 65.

Shute End: Nos. 1, 3, 4, 5, 8, 10a, 12, 14, 16.

Station Road: Hope & Anchor P.H.

Reading Road: The Clockhouse & Parish Rooms (although an older building, 1866, and also built by the Walters of Bearwood, the former St. Paul`s School is not listed.) No. 128 Ochiltree Cottage.

The Terrace: Nos. 3, 5, 7, 9, 11, 15 (said to be the oldest house in Wokingham, dating from the about c.1325 frontage much modernised.) Nos.17, 19, 21, 21a. No.23 Queens Head P.H. (the only building in Wokingham with a cruck frame.) Nos. 25, 29, 31, 33, 35, 37, 39, 41, 43, 45, 47.

Warren House Road: barn at Ashridge Farm south east of farmhouse, Cattle shed at Ashridge Farm north of farmhouse.

Wiltshire Road: Ashridge Cottage, Wiltshire Farmhouse, Nos. 2, 4, 6 (Tudor Corner and 96 Rose Street), No. 8 Richmond Cottage.

I have hopefully covered all the listed properties, but I expect that someone will tell me otherwise, so I apologise for any error or omission here and now.

The Latest Years

Some of this I have already touched upon, but life is still full of activity. Since I received the honour of becoming an Honorary Townsperson, I have become quite involved in work on committees at the Town Hall, and at one time quite committed to the Town Centre Management Initiative. In this body for some time were various small sub-committees dealing with various aspects of the town.

For instance, I was chairman of the environmental group which, amongst other things, was responsible for costing and positioning floral arrangements; agreeing the purchase and positioning of seats with sponsorship by Messrs. Waitrose—obviously with the consent of the W.D.C. Highways Dept.; locating the 'Welcome' sign near the Ship Inn on London Road, and the tarmac surface in Broad Street Walk. Financial support was provided by prominent local business men, and donations were made by most of the business people who use this roadway. The organisation of T.C.M.I. changed but still goes on with very worthwhile work.

Another important achievement was the provision of the first piece of public art in the town, namely the statue that graces the entrance to the library on the upper level. It had been planned to erect something at the lower entrance but as there are so many main services just below the surface, this was impracticable.

However, after much discussion, it was decided to follow up on the research of Barbara Young into the life and times of James Seaward, the local sweep. James had been a boy sweep in Victorian times when he was sent up the chimney with a hand-brush. In later years he would visit Charles Kingsley in Eversley, to sweep the chimneys at the Rectory,. Having related his experiences as a boy to the author, Kingsley included him as Tom the boy sweep in 'The Waterbabies'.

Angie Gibson, the then town centre manager, Councillor Tina Marinos and I visited the sculptress, Lydia Karpinska A. R. B. S., at her home to discuss the project. It was finally decided that the statue should depict two children sitting on the leaves of the book supported on its cover. A boy and girl—Tim Gardner and Kim White, were selected as models for the project. They visited the studio a number of times for Ms. Karpinska to create the images. Now, of course, they are immortalised in bronze.

There was a good gathering of James Seaward's relations, and many interested local people who attended the unveiling, which took place in June, 1999. It is to be hoped that further works of art can be sited in the town in the future.

I have had the pleasure of serving as Chairman of the Historic Sites & Buildings Working Party for a number of years. This group of very dedicated people does its utmost to protect the listed buildings in the town, and to elevate to listed building status those buildings which are considered to be important or in need of protection.

Another very interesting body that I have been a member of for many years is the Town Hall Development Committee. Many hours of discussion about this historic building have taken place over some years and a variety of opinions expressed. Everyone is working hard to achieve the right result with this jewel in the town's crown. It is now listed as Grade II* which gives it added protection. One of the very important objectives is now complete—access for disabled people. With the installation of a lift, a number of people have been able to visit the main hall for the first time.

It is common knowledge that there are other objectives to work for and it will steadily progress. However, it is a delicate balancing act and it is impossible to satisfy everyone. I have also been privileged to be on the panel for the Civic Awards.

The recent editions of the town guide is another project in which I have been pleased to be participating. The current edition is available in the Information Centre at the Town Hall—a really superb publication.

Another enjoyable pursuit in which I have been involved, in common with other members of the History Group, has been talking to many local people and encouraging them to talk into a microphone. I ask them questions and prompt them to dig deep into their memories. This results in some wonderful archival material recalling times past. Once started, these folk bring to mind all manner of events in which they have been involved. It is a sad fact of life that these memories will be lost forever if they are not on record. I hope to continue to be involved in this sort of service as long as I am able.

Both Edna and myself have been members of the Wokingham Society for some years,. Although we try to be supportive of this fine body it is to be regretted that time does not allow for more commitment.

In 1998 we were delighted and amazed to receive an invitation to an event that gave Edna and myself a great deal of pleasure. A visit to Buckingham Palace to enjoy the splendid delights of a Royal Garden Party. The date of this was 14th July, 1998.

We joined the masses of people to move through the Palace and into the gardens where we had complete freedom to walk around the grounds accompanied by the music of two military bands playing on the lawns. A long range of tents were ranged along one side of the lawns and a wide selection of wonderful food available served by dozens of the Palace staff.

Her Majesty and Prince Philip spent a long time speaking to many people and other members of the Royal Family were also in attendance. It was an occasion we shall remember all our days.

On 12th January, 2004 we travelled to Ocean Village, Southampton, boarded a Blue Funnel steamer and sailed out into Southampton Water. Here we witnessed the wonderful liner, Queen Mary 2 set off on her maiden voyage accompanied by an incredible firework display. A very spectacular event.

August 12th 1904 was the day of the final passing out parade of the Technical College at Arborfield Garrison. There was a magnificent display of precision marching to military bands. Many old boys of the college were present, including a Chelsea Pensioner. Edna and I felt privileged to be invited to attend such a memorable event.

oOo

In Conclusion.

For some years various people have coaxed or cajoled me to write about Wokingham. I have to admit that I have doubted my ability to do so. Perhaps this little volume has proved me to be right.

This book may be a huge disappointment to those who were expecting a detailed historical revue, but there is so much information available about the town that it would have been rather repetitive. Also, it has been said that when I 'pop off', everything I talk about during a "Wokingham Past & Present" show, would go with me. That is not the case for the reason I have just given. What will go of course are my personal memories, and that is what has mainly been the reason for my compiling this book. It may not be a contender for the "Booker Prize" but I hope you have enjoyed it anyway.

Thank you for your patience and endurance.

oOo

pto for Arnold's snippet.

and finally a Snippet from Dickie Arnold.

You have heard of
the man who called
His Goat "Nearly" because
it was All But.
His Cat "Whisky" because
it was Black & White.
His Dog "Sausage" because
it was Half Bred.
His Chicken "Robinson"
because it Crew So.
But have you heard of

R. ARNOLD,

The Interesting Shop,

Peach Street,

WOKINGHAM.

"Call" so that he may know you.
Phone 160.

The Shop front still stands and is part of
Marks and Spencer frontage.

126